RAISING YOUR
CHILDREN WITH
No Regrets

RAISING YOUR
CHILDREN WITH

No Regrets

7 Principles

of an

Intentional Mother

CATHERINE HICKEM L.C.S.W.

WINEPRESS **WP** PUBLISHING

WinePress Publishing (PO Box 428, Enumclaw, WA 98022) functions only as book publisher. As such, the ultimate design, content, editorial accuracy, and views expressed or implied in this work are those of the author.

Unless otherwise noted, all Scripture quotations are from the Holy Bible, New International Version, copyright © 1973, 1978, 1984 by the International Bible Society. Used by permission of Zondervan Publishing House. The "NIV" and "New International Version" trademarks are registered in the United States Patent and Trademark Office by International Bible Society.

Many names and circumstances within have been changed for the sake of privacy.

ISBN 13: 978-1-57921-888-1
ISBN 10: 1-57921-888-1
Library of Congress Catalog Card Number: 2007921238

Printed in Colombia.

DEDICATION

To my mother,

Mary Ann Taylor.

You are the greatest example of godly mothering
I've ever known,
and you first taught me that "no regret" motherhood is possible.

To my children,

Taylor and Tiffany Hickem.

You have been my passion and my heart, and you unleashed a
love in me I didn't know existed.

ACKNOWLEDGMENTS

I am thankful for . . .

. . . God, the Father of my faith, the source of my strength, and my reason for being. For Christ, who loved me enough to give up His own life for me and gave me the gift of eternity with Him. For the Holy Spirit, who is the best friend and source of wisdom, insight, and parenting advice I've ever had.

. . . my husband, Neil, who is my biggest fan and a great partner in parenting our children. Your gentle spirit, your sense of humor, and your behind-the-scenes support have allowed me to follow my passion for sharing Christ. I have loved you for thirty years, and I look forward to thirty more.

. . . my son, Taylor, whose miraculous entry into our lives healed my wounded heart and symbolized God's faithfulness. You have challenged me at every level, yet because of you, I know the bigness of God. I love you so much, and I am honored to be your mother.

. . . my daughter, Tiffany, whose miracle birth showed me once again the favor of the Lord. You bring out a side of me that no one else can touch. I love and adore you more than words can say.

. . . my parents, Harold and Mary Ann Taylor, who walked before me with lives of grace, integrity, and humility. You are the greatest examples of true Christianity I've ever seen, and I still can't believe you are my parents.

. . . the precious people who have served faithfully through CenterPeace Ministries, Kingdom Princess, and Intentional Motherhood. I am honored to have served with you through the years. You will never know how overwhelmed I am to have had the privilege to call you my friends.

. . . my personal prayer shield. Your faithfulness to pray for my family, this ministry, and me is a priceless gift. I will forever be indebted to you because you have prayed me through thick and thin for years. From the bottom of my heart, I love you!

. . . Pam, my steadfast assistant, who blesses me daily with her diligence, her commitment to excellence, and her wonderful servant heart.

. . . my editorial team:

- my editor, Janis Whipple, who has become a friend through the journey of this process;

- Karen Daniel, who has been that second set of eyes to critique and lend her expertise to the book;

- Susan Hagen, PhD, and Marie Rogers, PhD, my colleagues, who are the best examples of counsel and wisdom with which I've had the privilege to work . . .

  I say thank you for believing in me enough to help me articulate the heart of the Intentional Motherhood message with clarity, hope, faith, and truth.

. . . my friends and my church family, who have blessed me with love, prayed for me with faith, stood alongside me through adversity, and believed in the Christ in me. I say a grateful "thank you."

CONTENTS

Acknowledgments   vii
Foreword   xi
Preface   xv

Introduction   1
A Mother's Heart

Chapter 1   17
Why Well-Meaning Moms Raise Insecure Kids
    Principle 1: Be Intentional about
        Understanding Your Purpose

Chapter 2   43
Why Good Kids Don't Feel Good
    Principle 2: Be Intentional about
        Knowing Your Child

Chapter 3   65
You Can Live Peacefully in the Teenage Years
    Principle 3: Be Intentional about
        Being a Vision Keeper

Chapter 4   83
Become a Thinking Mom
    Principle 4: Be Intentional about
        Developing Emotional Intelligence

Chapter 5   107
Respect Is Necessary; Happiness Is Not
    Principle 5: Be Intentional about
        Maintaining Your Position

Chapter 6   129
The Difference between Control and Intention
    Principle 6: Be Intentional about
      Being Intentional

Chapter 7   149
God's Sense of Humor Begins with Contractions
    Principle 7: Be Intentional about
      Being God-Dependent

Conclusion   165
The Beginning and the End of the Story

Coaching Plan   173
Additional Resources   179
Endnotes   185
About the Author   187
Telling Your Stories   189

FOREWORD

Taylor:

When I was growing up, Mom usually had some idea as to what I was up to. Many times I hoped she'd take a vacation from being a mom for a while so I could really have fun. But she never did. Even so, at times she'd go easy on me when teaching me a lesson. The effect of her parenting came through without her being harsh about it.

Mom also placed a high value on spiritual growth—probably higher than anything else. She made sure church was a place I wanted to go. She demonstrated biblical principles and a moral basis for everyday life.

Mom's had many roles in my life, especially as a protector—protecting me from myself and others. She's always been supportive and good at adjusting to her new roles as they changed throughout my life. She was great at adapting to the new needs I had at each age. She knows that I now need a young adult's mom. She's always known her proper place in my life, despite where I was, how old I was, or who I was.

She always listened to me. She knew I was a night person, so she'd stay up way into the night, talking about any issue I had until I reached a resolution.

She always jumped into whatever I was doing, whether it was playing basketball or taking an English course. She always found a way to get into my life. But she wouldn't meddle, just be there. She showed me the importance of boundaries, and always respected my personal boundaries.

Kids start off as clay; they're very impressionable. Moms don't get second chances; they have to do it right the first time. I'm grateful my mom got it right.

Tiffany:

Mom has often said we make her look good. Yet as flattered as we are to receive such a compliment, we see things a little differently. If we had a dollar for every time someone told us they loved our mom, we'd be able to buy an island. Well, actually, Taylor would invest the money in a high-yield mutual fund, but I would definitely look into that island!

By the time you finish this book you will know why so many people love my mom. Here are a few of my reasons:

She's a parenting genius. Plain and simple, she's one of the wisest people I know. (And I'm not just saying this because I take after her!) She really knows exactly what to do in any situation, with any problem, about anything.

She is who she appears to be. The mom that speaks at national conferences is the same as the one who speaks when just the two of us are having dinner or driving in the car. She doesn't change for her audience, because she doesn't need to.

She's funny. Despite its serious subject, this book is sure to make you laugh at times. Taylor and I provided Mom with many comedic moments throughout our lives. Most of the time she laughed with us; the rest of the time she laughed at us. But she was able to find a sense of humor in the midst of difficulty.

She doesn't pretend to have all the answers. But she knows the One who does. When approached with a problem, she first and foremost looks at what is biblical and Christlike. She exemplifies a life where God is both her partner and her authority.

There are many more reasons and ways I love my mom than I could ever possibly put into words. She is my mentor, protector, nurturer, teacher, encourager, and best friend. She has more insight and wisdom to offer than anyone I know. After you read her words, I hope you find a depth of friendship and love with your child that my mom has with me. It is truly the most rewarding relationship I have in my life.

⁕

We welcome you to read this book, take a glimpse into our lives, and learn from our mom's wisdom. Our hope is that you close this book changed, with a deeper understanding of yourself, your children, and our God.

We hope you appreciate our mom as much as we do.

—Taylor and Tiffany Hickem

PREFACE

Dear Moms,

Over the years, I've read many books on motherhood, parenting, and children. I found many of them to be a blessing and typically took a nugget of wisdom from everything I read.

So the question arises, "Why write another book on motherhood?"

Most of the books I read were designed *for* the mother and failed to mention that motherhood is also *about* the mother. *You* are the core to a child's development; to pay attention to your role only through the eyes of a child shortchanges your child.

I wanted this book to be about *you*!

I want you to clearly see how God had you in mind when He created your children. I want you to recognize the power you have in the unfolding lives of your children. I want you to see the importance of living in integrity before your children so you can have the respect, trust, faith, and influence a mother needs to parent her children with no regrets.

Finally, I want you to recognize the power of partnering with Christ in mothering your kids. He intentionally chose to reveal

Himself to you through them. While He is wild about your kids, He is just as passionate about you.

You will learn a lot about your children in the following pages, but I believe you will learn even more about yourself. The more you know who God is in your life, the better you will be able to pass His wisdom down to the next generation.

From one mom to another,

Catherine

Luke 12:48

A MOTHER'S HEART

On the center of my business card is a lime green dash—stark, clean, and neat. The Dash Organization is the name of my secular business, but more than that, it explains my life. The dash is who I am. Its simplicity captures the essence of me.

I chose a dash to provoke questions.

I first heard about the dash idea from my friend Phil, my children's principal at the time. Before a new academic year began, he was diagnosed with a malignant tumor. He took the year off to battle cancer, but kept his position and came back to speak at graduation.

At the commencement ceremony, Phil read a poem entitled "The Dash" by Linda Ellis.[1] Perhaps you've heard it before. The poem reminds us that when we die, the date of our birth and death are listed, while the little symbol between the dates is often ignored—the dash.

How simple.

"People won't remember the dates of your birth and death but what you did with the time in between," Phil reminded us all.

How profound!

Along my own journey, the dash has often challenged me.

How will my life matter?

How will I be remembered?

Still, something bothered me. I needed to answer another question first:

Who do I want to impact?

In whose life can I make the greatest difference?

Who—not *how*—was where I needed to begin. My challenge to live a memorable life during my dash would be simpler if I prioritized my impact.

This challenge began with those closest to me. Naturally, as a woman, it revolved around the lives I had been entrusted with—my children.

While I know that I also carry great responsibility in my relationship with my husband, Neil, that's a different type of relationship and responsibility. Adults walk into a relationship with some idea of the other person's personality and character. This provides a foundation for relating to each other.

Children are a different story.

For most of us, children enter our lives tiny and dependent—completely reliant upon us to care for them in every way. Before our baby is born, we have no idea what type of child we're getting.

Boy or girl?

Athletic or artistic?

Reserved or outgoing?

Questions, questions, questions. Some answers come quickly (boy or girl?) and some take a lifetime. Our children constantly evolve and unfold as they grow; that is their role in our lives.

Yet the issue isn't about them; it's about us, their mothers.

What is our job?

If your answer to the question, "Who do I want to impact?" is, "My children," you must first know what influence you want to have on them and how to go about it. You can't just "go with the flow" and then cross your fingers and hope they turn out okay.

You and I need to believe that a lifetime invested in our children will reap a great value. To have the highest impact, we must start our mothering journey with an intentional plan.

Several years ago, my friend Diana and I went to Atlanta to attend a dear friend's wedding. Another friend, Suzanne, who lived in the Atlanta suburbs, had given me a key to her home to use as my own when I traveled in the area. Although on this particular weekend Suzanne would be out of town, Diana and I still planned to stay at her home.

I assured Diana I would have no problem locating Suzanne's home because I had stayed there so many times. Although a year had passed since my last visit to Suzanne's, I was quite confident we would have no trouble finding our way.

Did you notice I was *confident*?

As I drove toward Suzanne's community, I passed several areas that looked familiar. My confidence remained intact.

As I approached the interstate exits, however, things looked less familiar. Was it exit 102 or 106? How about exit 105? That number had a ring to it.

We got off and on one exit after another, looking for landmarks to finally point me in the direction of Suzanne's house. As we drove, I began to realize that in the year since I had been in the area, many new developments had popped up.

Additional buildings altered the terrain.

New strip malls replaced previous shopping centers.

Landscaping completely changed the feel of the community.

What I was so confident of a year earlier was no longer the same.

Fortunately, Diana was used to my adventures. Having traveled thousands of miles with me all across the country, she'd learned to go with the flow. Better yet, she still had a sense of humor at 1:00 A.M. when we pulled into a fire station to ask for help.

Diana and I still laugh about that evening. The worst-case scenario would have been that we had to find a hotel. No big deal in the overall scheme of life, thankfully.

The task was simple: I thought I knew where I was going, but by the time I got there I was lost.

Things changed, and I didn't keep pace with the changes. I didn't plan my trip with the attention to detail that would have made it less stressful and more enjoyable.

My Atlanta experience is exactly like motherhood when we don't become *intentional* about our plans for parenting our children. We may begin our road to motherhood with a sense of confidence, but by the time our children become adults, we may feel lost, sad, guilty, or full of regret.

We may reach our general destination, but we can't achieve the full potential of our parenting if we (and our children) don't arrive where our heart truly desired.

The saddest part is that God never intended for mothers to live with such regret, doubt, and self-condemnation. While mothering is the hardest job we'll ever undertake, our Creator designed it to be the most rewarding, most powerful, and closest to grasping God's heart of any relationship in our lives.

No Regrets

On August 14, 2003, my husband and I had just finished unloading all our son's things in his dorm room at Georgia Tech. Everything was set up; we'd had lunch—all that was left was good-bye.

While a part of my heart had always dreaded this moment—leaving my firstborn behind—another part was relieved. We had prayer, said good-bye, hugged Taylor one last time, and walked out of his room. As we left, in my mind I saw myself hand the baton back to God, and I said to Him, "Taylor really is all yours now."

As I drove away, I realized I had no regrets.

Now, understand something. This was a powerful moment for me.

Notice that I didn't say "no mistakes." There had been plenty of those on my part. But mistakes and regret are two different things.

Raising Taylor had been like giving birth to broken dishes every day of my life. Nothing was simple or easy about my firstborn son. He was thought-provoking, complex, challenging, interesting. Taylor definitely didn't march to anyone else's drummer. My son caused me to be prostrate more times than upright. He challenged my intellectual capacity, emotional stability, and spiritual maturity every day.

Though he overwhelmed me daily, at the same time he taught me more than anyone else in my life. Through all that, motherhood taught me how to be God-dependent rather than self-reliant. So by the time I left my son at college that day, I truly walked away with no regrets.

You, too, can raise your children with no regrets . . .

. . . if you become an intentional mother.

MOTHERING WITHOUT REGRET

Unfortunately, too many moms send their young adult children out into the world and then experience an overwhelming sense of regret. They wonder: *Are my kids ready for the world? Did I teach them the right things? What if I made a bad decision that affects them forever? What could I have done differently?*

You can, however, reach that day when you wave your children good-bye and send them off without such questions.

The *American Heritage Dictionary* defines *regret* as "to remember with a feeling of loss or sorrow"; "a feeling of disappointment or distress about something that one wishes could be different." This definition of *regret* includes anguish, woe, heartache, and heartbreak. *Regret* is one of several nouns denoting mental distress, and it has the broadest range—from mere disappointment to a painful sense of self-reproach or dissatisfaction, as over something lost or done.[2]

Every mother fears that she'll spend twenty years of her life raising her child only to discover that she missed investing in and teaching the things that mattered.

Even if your children are still in process when they enter adulthood, it is possible to release them to the world and to know you don't regret anything about the way you raised them.

If you've been intentional along the way.

To arrive at the motherhood destination we desire, you and I must choose to be intentional about our children and their lives. This choice may look different from what you initially imagined, so give yourself permission to think outside the box.

This book is your call to action.

I will ask you to think differently than you're accustomed and to believe you have the ability to rise to the occasion. I will ask you to lay down any expectations about what you think this book might say.

This book will challenge you, comfort you, convict you, and empower you.

This book will ask you to think, question, dream, and plan.

MOTHERHOOD GOALS

Everything important in life requires planning. Weddings, academic degrees, and careers—all encompass a large degree of planning. Each life-determining goal has a purpose tailored to meet the needs of the individual or couple.

We set a goal, and then invest time, energy, and money to achieve it. Markers along the way keep us on track to ensure we accomplish our goal. We follow our plan and adapt as needs arise or our desires change.

When we understand our purpose and direction in life, we demonstrate more confidence, exert more energy, possess more hope, set bigger goals, and experience a greater sense of accomplishment. We're more likely to hang in there when things get tough because we know the current state eventually will change.

We don't give up easily.

We're confident.

When it comes to our kids, however, we seem to meander through their childhood and adolescence instead of determining goals in this arena with *intention*, as with other important missions in our lives. The principles that help us achieve greatness in careers, events, personal goals, or even marriage are often absent in the most significant undertaking in our lives—the formation and development of our children.

When you ask a new mother about her hopes and goals for her children, she usually says she wants her children to grow up to be happy, confident, emotionally healthy people with meaningful, productive lives. Yet it doesn't dawn on her—or any of us for that matter—that just because she *desires* meaningful lives for her children doesn't guarantee it will automatically happen.

We must give purposeful thought to our desires.

We must put actions to our goals.

We must set our sights on delayed gratification while we do the work now.

We must be *intentional*!

For years, motherhood as a role has carried wide expectations but little direction on how to do it well. Many moms enter this significant responsibility with few goals and purposes, simply trying to get through each day with as few crises as possible.

We enter motherhood with our dreams, ideals, and desires.

It begins the day we discover we're going to become a mother. But our dreams and desires can easily be dashed by reality—and our hearts broken—if we're not prepared to intentionally raise our children with specific purposes and goals.

MOTHERHOOD IS MORE

Motherhood is more than feeding, holding, diapering.

Motherhood is more than helping our children learn to crawl, walk, and feed themselves.

Motherhood is more than simply going through the motions.

Motherhood encompasses the critical season when children make attachments of security, learn how to trust, and incorporate the value of boundaries. During their early years, your children begin to recognize they are valuable and their needs matter. Motherhood isn't so much about you as it is about your kids developing a sense of emotional and physical safety that will set a foundation for how they perceive the world.

Your failure to learn these critical issues during your child's first years can result in lifelong struggles and difficulties for them. If you don't recognize the significance of this season of development, you might undermine your child's potential and consequently face difficult, complex problems later.

Are you overwhelmed yet?

It gets better. I promise.

A new season of mothering begins when your kids hit around age eight. At this time, the issues change because the basic path of your kids' personalities is already largely formed. You begin to recognize who your children are and who they are not. Their interests, talents, and abilities start to emerge during this season of development.

Learning disabilities also can surface at this time, as can social and emotional problems, if they haven't already. You must seize this season of your children's lives because this is the time to instill beliefs, convictions, and principles. How are you doing in this area? How do you know if your children grasp your values?

This season is also the most critical for establishing a strong sense of identity, confidence, and critical thinking skills. *Before* the rush of hormones is the time for mothers to teach healthy definitions of male/female relationships, sexuality, purity, and respect.

Yet childhood is easy compared to the turmoil of the next phase . . .

Middle school.

The "tween" years pose new challenges. Reputation and rumors implant fear and trembling in even the most confident moms as they anticipate this phase of motherhood. True, this phase is difficult, but not for the reasons you suspect.

Let's be honest.

You've heard awful stories about fifth-to-eighth-grade children.

> You've been told they are unpredictable, strange, and weird.

>> Have you been looking forward to this age with excitement and wonder?

Probably not!

Forget all the horror stories about this phase of your child's life and begin to recognize that God's mysteries and sense of humor often reveal themselves during this age. This phase is another way for God to get our attention, because during this season mothers truly recognize how badly they need His help. Children in this age range are scared, awkward, impulsive, and insecure about every part of who they are. Too many mothers listen to other mothers instead of recognizing their children's stage of need and development.

The key is for you not to wig out but to understand.

The way you handle the middle-school years will either bond you and your child together or separate your hearts. In working with children and families for twenty-five years, I've found that by the time a child is fourteen, or near the end of his or her eighth-grade year, the learning window will close. Whatever you have poured into them to this point will surface (or not) during the next phase of their lives. In addition, their peers will begin to exert a larger influence on their lives. So if you're intentional during the middle-school years, you will lay a great foundation for the next phase.

So are you ready for adolescence?

How do the high-school years grab you?

Do you like what you see in your children at this point?

Adolescence is a difficult time for your children because their minds are still vulnerable and they face increased challenges with their emotions and bodies. The tension between their moral values and their changing bodies comes into play. They struggle to figure out who they are, how they fit in, and what they believe.

High-school teens are faced with significant life decisions and don't always possess the self-awareness to handle themselves well in tight situations.

- They doubt whether they're acceptable.
- They question if anyone will ever love them.
- They feel alone and overwhelmed.
- They ask themselves:

What should I do with my life? Who will I become?

Do I like myself? Do others like me?

Where will I go to college? How will I make a living?

Does this endless stream of questions and comments overwhelm and scare you? I hope so.

I want you to understand the cost to your children if you simply go through the motions of motherhood without engaging your mind, seeking God's guidance, and being intentional about how you mother them. A mother has a lot to lose if she is only a *maintenance* mom—one who goes through the daily, surface routines of life with no thought of the long-term implications of her decisions, the depth of her role as mother, and the power of the moment. Failure to grasp that she's instilling values, forming definitions of relationships, and establishing the relevancy of faith in Christ in her children's lives will lead her to many regrets when her kids launch into the world.

If you don't engage your emotional intelligence during this journey—if you don't *think* about the implications of your daily reactions and decisions—your children will suffer. If you don't include God in your motherhood journey, your children won't have a foundation of spiritual values on which to learn to make their own decisions. Worse yet, if you fail to develop your children's emotional intelligence and sense of faith, they may fail in the areas of life that matter most.

The good news—yes, there's good news!—is that during the teen years you begin to see the investments you made in their earlier years pay off.

You will be tested, tortured, and teased.

> You will live through it.

>> You will be the better person for it . . . if you have been *intentional*.

Your life will be richer for experiencing these years with your children, and the potential bond between you will be unbelievable.

According to Webster's dictionary, the word *intent* means to have one's attention sharply focused or fixed on something. This clearly describes God's heart for humanity when He created us. He had a plan that focused on creating beings for relationship with Him—people who would bring Him honor.

God was intentional in everything He created, planned, and loved.

This book will show you the ways of God, the First Parent—the ultimate parent. You will discover the steadfastness with which you can be the intentional mother God desired you to be and modeled for you as an example.

Intentional Motherhood Principles

As the title states, there are *seven* principles of *intentional motherhood*. Let me outline them for you.

1. *The first principle* is that mothers must be intentional about their *purpose*. In a day and age when so many well-meaning mothers raise insecure kids, mothers must be willing to stop and examine the reasons they do what they do. This principle brings mothers face-to-face with the power they have in their children's lives and development. This chapter outlines the importance of living in integrity and encourages you to assess how you view yourself.

2. *The second principle* is an invitation for mothers to be intentional about *knowing their children*. This chapter explains why "good" kids don't often feel good about themselves. We'll discuss the assumptions we make about what our children actually believe about themselves and the struggles that interfere with their confidence, value, and potential. You'll discover how being an intentional mother can eliminate most turmoil when you understand what truly *knowing* your children means. You'll be empowered to know how to communicate powerful truths to your children.

3. *The third principle* teaches mothers to be intentional by *keeping the vision* for their children, keeping the end in mind. In other words, this chapter teaches you how to live peacefully through your child's teenage years. The tenets

for being able to do this begin when your children are young. However, it's never too late to learn the truths that give you hope, heart, and faith during a time when young adults are faced with their greatest challenges. Reframing the significance of mistakes from God's perspective helps you breathe deeply when you might otherwise rant. This chapter is a must for scared moms.

4. *The fourth principle* introduces the need for mothers to help their children develop *emotional intelligence*, including learning to identify feelings. You'll learn the importance of thinking through situations, and of teaching your children the same. This chapter illustrates the impact on your children if you neglect this area of your heart and theirs. You'll discover the tools for learning to be insightful, sensitive, and connected to your children.

5. *The fifth principle* challenges mothers to be intentional about *maintaining their position*—their authority and influence. This chapter helps you understand the key differences between respect and happiness, illustrating how the former is necessary and the latter is not. One of the single greatest mistakes today's mothers make is the failure to understand the difference between these two unique concepts. Mothers must recognize the damage caused when they don't have a handle on the rightful place of respect and happiness in their motherhood.

6. *The sixth principle* asks mothers to be intentional about *being intentional*. This chapter delves into the vast difference between being a controlling mother and one who is intentional. It outlines the impact of each approach on your efforts to build trust, faith, and emotional health in your children.

7. *The seventh principle* exhorts mothers to be intentional about *being God-dependent*. God's sense of humor begins with contractions. Whether adoption or natural birth, we

really have no control as to when our baby will arrive. It is out of our hands from the beginning; this is God's first lesson in motherhood. This chapter will focus on teaching you how to rely on and trust the One who created your children.

While this book is primarily for you moms, dads will be blessed when you embrace an intentional approach to mothering. This allows the father of your children to feel more comfortable in his role as a dad. Men are more confident when there's a plan of action and a sense of direction. When a father recognizes the significance of being intentional with his children's lives—by seeing his children's mother setting the example—he will more likely take this challenge seriously and participate more actively.

THINKING IN A NEW DIRECTION

When my friend Diana and I got lost on our trip, it reminded me how easily we can be *confidently* deceived. My experience that evening didn't have life-threatening implications for me and my friend. However, a lost and undirected mother can experience unfortunate and disastrous results with her most precious treasures.

Are you a mother who doesn't want to get lost on her way to rearing healthy children?

Is your mother's heart full of dreams for your children to grow into adults with the character, value, and faith to positively impact their world?

Are you ready to be a mother who lives with no regrets?

Would you like to truly trust God with your children?

Then join me as we travel together down an intentional road that God Himself has gently prepared for us.

But be ready: as you read, there will be moments when you want to put the book down.

Do so.

Question what I say.

Disagree and struggle if you want.

But if it makes you think, then I have accomplished the heart of this book.

Do not passively embark on this motherhood journey without knowing where you're going and why you seek a particular destination. For your children's sake, be present and aware for the most significant contribution you will ever make: the formation of a life!

FAITH POINTS

From everyone who has been given much,
much will be demanded; and from the one who has been
entrusted with much, much more will be asked.

~ Luke 12:48 ~

Have you ever viewed your children as gifts God has entrusted to you? This Scripture says that if we've been given much, much will be expected. Think through the following questions in light of this verse:

1. If God has trusted you with your children, what do you think it says about His opinion of you?

2. If "much more" is asked of those who've been entrusted with much, what "much more" is God asking of you as a mother?

WHY WELL-MEANING MOMS RAISE INSECURE KIDS

Principle 1: Be Intentional about Understanding Your Purpose

During my early years as a pastor's wife, I often volunteered in the church nursery. I saw every possible type of new mom walk through those nursery doors, and I learned a few things.

New moms don't realize it, but they can set up their little ones for later anxiety issues simply by how they leave their young ones in the nursery—or the day care, or with a friend or family member. Let me explain.

Every child has initial issues with separation anxiety. It's a natural transition with babies. When infants are separated from Mom, they may be unhappy about being left with someone they don't know well. They will cling, cry, and scream. But the truth is, they won't be damaged, traumatized, or permanently scarred.

Nine times out of ten, they calm down once they're distracted or comforted.

The lessons they learn are:

> they're safe,
>
> Mommy will come back,
>
> and they can trust Mommy to leave them with someone who will take care of them.

If a mother's own anxiety surfaces about leaving her child, I can assure you that her child senses it. Children are born sensors, so they know when Mom is upset. This inadvertently sends a message to the little one: *If Mommy is nervous, maybe I'm not safe.*

Nothing is wrong with moms keeping an eye on their child's adjustment to change or new environments. However, the real issue isn't the child's ability to adjust but the mom's own discomfort, fear, and anxiety that her child senses.

Are these well-meaning moms? Absolutely!

Are they wonderful, terrific people? No doubt!

Will they contribute to making their children insecure or anxious about trying new things in the future? Yes!

Is that their heart? Not at all.

Mom, that's why this first principle—purpose—is more about you than your children. So I have to get personal. And because nothing is more personal than being a mother, let's hit the issue head-on so you can be the best mom your children deserve.

Now, no pressure, but *you are the single most significant female your child will ever know*. Regardless of how *you* feel about your importance, you must begin to immediately recognize your value in the eyes of your child. Failure to grasp this concept has a cost.

It will cost your child his or her self-worth.

It will cost you peace of mind and heart.

It will cost the Kingdom the opportunity to be as blessed as God intended.

That's a high price to pay simply because we *wander* through motherhood instead of moving *intentionally* with purpose.

Over the years, a mother's importance has become obscured. I've often compared the awareness of motherhood to grout in a kitchen floor: no one notices it until it's gone. Yet as the significance of motherhood fell into obscurity, our role became more complex with greater demands. Every mother at one time or another feels the burden that comes with those expectations. Often mothers give so much with so little regard.

Cultural assumptions add to the stress. It seems society equates our biological ability to give birth with the ability to be a good mother. The truth is, thousands of women bring children successfully into the world every day. But it takes a special woman with focus and intention to successfully raise her children. The position of "mother" is taken less and less seriously in our society; instead, the significance of motherhood should be greeted with the highest respect.

Unfortunately for our children, we mothers have bought into our culture's diminished view of our role because we underestimate our importance to our children. If we were truly conscious of our influence, many of the critical issues in the lives of today's kids would not exist, and I wouldn't be writing this book.

What Is a Mom's Purpose?

I want you to stop reading for a moment and go get a sheet of paper and pencil. Now take a few minutes to write down what you believe your purpose is in being a mother. Give yourself some time to reflect. Make it a sentence or two, and remember, this isn't a test. When you're done, lay it aside.

That was difficult, wasn't it?

Asking you to state your purpose as a mother is like asking you to give the history of the world in thirty words or less. Motherhood is a concept everyone believes in but few can articulate. One of the reasons we struggle with its description is that the list of roles within the role never ends.

The other problem is that while we can describe the *tasks* of our position, we struggle to articulate the intangible *heart* of mothering children. And if we can't express our purpose, even to ourselves, the likelihood of living it out is slim.

A 2005 study on motherhood surveyed 2,009 moms across all demographic lines, with surprisingly similar responses in many areas. When asked if being a mother was "the most important thing I do," 81 percent said it was, and the remaining 19 percent said it was "one of several important things I do."[1] These moms also universally found satisfaction in being a mom (81 percent were very satisfied and 16 percent were somewhat satisfied) despite variance in their socioeconomic circumstances.[2]

The mothers surveyed obviously feel a strong sense of purpose in their role. So if we find such satisfaction and significance as moms, shouldn't we be confident in what our purpose is? Let's start by defining *purpose*.

A purpose is a reason, principle, or rationale for accomplishing something with meaning or value. It indicates that something has significance and depth and will require thought and attention to fulfill.

Now let's see how that applies to us.

A mother's purpose is influenced by background, history, and personality. It's also impacted by a woman's own personal journey with her mother. Therefore our definition of "normal motherhood" is based on how we were raised, because our mothers are our definition of "normal."

(I'm not saying every mother is healthy and worthy of modeling. What I am saying is that how we're raised as children defines "normal" for us until we learn what behaviors might not be normal after all.)

Even later, as mothers themselves, women look to their own mothers for emotional support. The study on motherhood also found that while "mothers most often named their spouse as their primary source of emotional support [48 percent] . . . 20 percent named their own mother."[3]

Think about this: *You represent what normal is to your children.*

> Your daughters likely will mother as you mother.

> Your sons likely will expect their wives to mother the way you did.

Do you need to think about this motherhood thing just a little more? Only if you don't want your job to come back and haunt you!

A mother's purpose is to give all of herself to uniquely impart values, faith, beliefs, and love into the children with whom she's been entrusted. Embrace the journey of motherhood with the belief that you will empower your children to fulfill the purpose of their creation. *Mothering with purpose is to recognize that your very existence defines love, gives life, protects innocence, believes in the impossible, and views life's struggles as opportunities to enrich your children's lives.*

The motherhood study confirms that mothers sense the significance of this support and nurture in the lives of their children: "Many women talked about mothers as the foundation of a child's sense of security and trust."[4]

A mother knows she is the emotional floor her children will build their lives on until they can transfer that foundation onto God.

This definition is overwhelming.

Some of you may think, *I may as well give up now, because there's no way I can be this kind of purposeful mom.*

Guess what?

You're right.

There's absolutely no way any woman can possibly meet this definition of a purposeful mother.

The good news is that God doesn't expect you to pull this off alone. He knows you're in over your head from the start. After all, He created you for this purpose. He wants you to understand the significance of your journey and not take it for granted. He wants you to catch a glimmer of the importance of this job you have undertaken; after all, you will symbolize God to your children. Their lives depend on you getting clued in so you can see the awesome responsibility, honor, and significance of your place in their lives.

When a mother knows her purpose, her children will know theirs. They will develop an inner sense that gives them internal and external confidence. They will be comfortable in their own skin and free to walk to the drummer's beat inside their heart; and hopefully that beat will come from God. They won't be so vulnerable to the demands of our culture because they will be less likely to view their peers as the definition of success. They will be grounded by the foundation of a mother's purposeful love, and not pounded by the world's ruthless expectations.

Isn't this what you want for your children? Having a purpose in your mothering will achieve this kind of life for them.

So what does a purposeful mother look like?

How do you become a mother who knows where she is going?

TRUST YOUR INTUITION

When we begin the journey of motherhood, we're often anxious. Do you remember how it felt the first time you became a mother?

I do.

We were adopting our first child, and had been waiting for our son to be born. Our attorney was concerned the birth mother might not go through with the adoption. Until the papers were signed, we knew that at any moment we might be left with empty arms and broken hearts.

Can you say "nerve-racking"?

Finally we took home our new adopted son, Taylor. I was both scared and excited. My husband, Neil, and I had waited a long time for a child, and I wanted to do things right. I look back now and see how overly protective I was for the first several weeks, especially since it appeared we might have a few medical concerns.

As time went on, I felt normal again. (I know. *Normal* has a broad definition.)

You can probably relate. The normal experience of being initially anxious as a new mom quickly disappears as we become increasingly familiar with our child. In those early years, we seem to manage pretty well as long as our offspring are strolling along normal paths of development. We hold on to our influence and position with relative ease. The only time we typically relinquish it is to a pediatrician or significant family member.

However, as our child enters formal education in kindergarten or first grade, we increasingly relinquish our instincts, observations, and knowledge. The process begins slowly, but by the time our child has reached middle school, our exasperation with them at this age fans the flames of inadequacy, further causing us to check our brains in at the door of anyone who appears to know more than we do. By the time this has occurred, our confidence is shaken, and we are vulnerable to doubt and criticism.

We wonder if we know what we're doing. We have trouble discerning between normal middle-school behavior and problem behavior. We think, *Maybe my child has a bigger issue than I'm equipped to handle.* We quietly question our own judgment about our children, and think others might be able to do for our child what we can't. As a result, our child responds with increased insecurity.

Sound familiar?

Do you see how easily the transition from confident to shaky can take place? Do you see how our children's confidence is also affected?

This happens because moms get caught up in what others think instead of what they know. This is one of the first major traps to avoid. We don't want to unknowingly slip into insecurity. And we won't if we are purposeful.

A purposeful mother understands that she doesn't possess all wisdom and knowledge about motherhood, children, and parenting.

However, what you do possess is the heart knowledge about your children, which will help you do what needs to be done when the time comes. As a purposeful mother, you know you are truly the expert on your children, and no one can replace you.

Do you get that?

You are the expert on your child!

When you seek outside counsel, it should be with the intent of seeking other options, answers, and possibilities to supplement, not replace, your own understanding. Listen to the wisdom of others with an intuitive heart and discerning mind. Trust that you will have peace when you have found the answer to your question. Then you will live with a quiet confidence that says you and God will get through the challenge of motherhood together. Trust your instincts as God's way of whispering in your ear His wisdom for your child.

Let me be clear about something here. Though we listen to and apply God's wisdom for our children, they still might make mistakes from time to time. Our children make choices that may go against our heart's desire for them, but that doesn't diminish our motherhood. And it doesn't mean that we're not listening to God or that He's not listening to us. God is bigger than our children's choices.

I recently counseled a Christian mother I had met years before when working part-time as an elementary school guidance counselor. I had observed her oldest daughter in the third grade and noticed she seemed a little unique. Yet I kept these thoughts to myself because the girl was performing well in class and not demonstrating any problem behaviors. Her mother never mentioned anything to me, so I didn't feel it was appropriate to point out her child's differences when there seemed to be no problem.

Fast-forward five years to this mother sitting in my office. Her daughter is about to enter high-school, but the remainder of her eighth-grade year bodes disaster.

The mother is a wreck.

The daughter is disconnected.

No one is happy!

"I've had this kid in therapy for years and she's been on medication for five years," Jean[5] began. "Something is wrong, but I can't put my finger on it. No one seems to hear me when I say that something is missing. Am I nuts or do you see what I mean?"

This was a mother in full-blown crisis mode. I proceeded to tell Jean my observations about her daughter years before, and I assured Jean I did not think she was crazy. I didn't have a diagnosis for her daughter at the time, but I absolutely knew this mother's instincts for her child were right on target.

Jean knew her daughter.

She also knew something wasn't right.

Jean had experienced a difficult relationship with her own mother, having been abandoned during her prepubescent years. She worked diligently not to repeat her mom's mistakes and was doing many wonderful things as a mother with her children.

Most importantly, Jean lived in integrity as a mother. She was a tender, spiritually minded woman who sought God's heart throughout her journey. Jean's problem is similar to that of many mothers. She sought help but didn't listen to the right voice. She believed God wanted the best for her daughter, but she didn't always trust the wisdom she received from Him. Had Jean listened to God's Spirit within her, she would have found the help her daughter needed earlier.

Some of you might be asking, "Well, if a mother's intuition comes from God, then what about those people who don't know God? How do they have instincts like those who do believe in Him?"

The answer is simple.

Maternal instinct is a gift He gives all women when they become mothers so they can properly care for their young.

If you doubt this, study the animal kingdom and observe how the behavior of a mother animal changes when her babies are born. God gave instincts to animals because He knew their young would need special care during their vulnerable, formative years.

Their Creator is our Creator.

After Jean and I talked, she went on to have her daughter evaluated by a professional I respected. The results validated Jean's gnawing instincts.

Something indeed was abnormal about her daughter.

If it had been properly diagnosed years earlier, the treatment intervention would have been less intense and the damage to her daughter less severe.

Yet in the midst of this difficult news, Jean felt restored and re-lieved. "I'm so grateful to know the truth," she said. "All these years I didn't have the answers I needed to meet my daughter's issues, so I thought it was just me. Now that I know, I can throw my heart and soul into giving my daughter what she needs."

Jean could be the poster child for mothers who don't trust their intuition to the point of action. She would be the first to tell you that one of the side effects of her journey is the insecurity result-ing from all the lost time.

Her greatest mistake was that she lost sight of her purpose and her voice. She failed to recognize that her perceptions and dis-cernment about her daughter were part of her purpose. It's every mother's job to be the voice for her child's needs and to raise her voice until it is heard, so answers and solutions can be found.

The good news is that even though it took her awhile, Jean did not turn a deaf ear to God.

Thank God she did not quit.

While the jury is still out on her daughter's journey, I'm confi-dent it has a much better probability of turning out better than it would have had Jean given up.

Maybe your face could be on that poster as well. Perhaps you have gnawing feelings about your child but no one has validated them for you. If this is the case, trust that God has placed those intuitive feelings inside you for a purpose; you simply haven't found the right person to help you.

God loves you and your children too much to leave a problem un-attended. Sometimes it may take a long, drawn-out process to get to the bottom of an issue, but don't give up. Your child will only benefit from your persevering effort. Your tenacity also communicates to your child the depth of his or her value and importance in your life. It's a win-win situation for all involved.

RECOGNIZE YOUR VALUE

The issue of our value is a sensitive one for most of us. This is where mothers of all ages start to squirm, tune out, or struggle.

Whether you do one or the other, or all three for that matter, I encourage you to stick with me. And you might want to highlight this section for future reference because I'm sure you'll want to return to it during times of struggle with your kids.

So here are the questions:

- Why should your value matter to you as a mom?

- Why is it so important to your children?

In the motherhood study I referred to earlier, 93 percent of those surveyed believed "Mothers see their contributions to the care of their children not only as extremely important, but also so unique that no one else can replace it."[6] While we know we are significant, we undermine our purpose by not recognizing the importance our presence brings to our children. Great moms recognize that there's a connection between their self-perception and their children's. As moms go, so go the kids. Still, we often take ourselves for granted until something severe happens; then we finally appreciate the power of our presence in our children's lives.

Several female friends of mine have died leaving children behind. These friends were precious women who loved life, God, and their families. They were wonderful moms who understood the privilege of being a mother. Their children knew they were safe and secure in their mother's arms.

In those moments of harsh reality, we see the gaping hole a mother's loss leaves. Regardless of how loved children are by their fathers, grandparents, surrounding relatives, and friends, the depth of pain those children experienced takes the air out of the room. I've personally found the pain almost unbearable. The touch that only a mother can give leaves an ache in the heart of her children that will never be filled. It is sad that too often we only appreciate a mother's presence when we're forced to experience the emptiness her absence leaves.

Now that I have you depressed and weeping, I want you to think about something: Has it ever dawned on you how much your children truly need you? Have you ever realized how your children long for your approval? Think about the following:

- When your children are in elementary school, do you notice how excited they get when you agree to chaperone a field trip or participate as a room mother?

- Do you notice that you're the first one they want to tell when they get an award or special attention?

- Are you aware of how your children will look for you—when they are performing on stage or on the ball field—to see how you're responding to their "time to shine" moment?

- When your child does something really awful, do you ever stop to notice how scared they are that they disappointed you?

All of these experiences reflect your significance to your child.

No one, and I mean *no one*, has the power you do.

This statement doesn't undermine the importance of dads. The two roles simply are different, not one less than the other.

Fathers play an extremely important role in the life of a child. He is the child's first definition of what a man is, what protection looks and feels like, and the example of what strong and soft look like in one package. Dads also are critical in a child's formation of faith, and they communicate an important understanding of how to treat others.

In the initial stages of a child's life, however, fathers are the second person on whom a child depends. Scripture demonstrates the mother as primary caretaker and nurturer. I love the story in 2 Kings 4 where the little boy has gone to work with his dad, but the minute he gets sick, the father says, "Carry him to his mother!"

By virtue of creation and pregnancy, the mother has the privilege and responsibility for the initial nurturing of her child. While her child is in the womb, a mother talks to her baby as she strokes her own stomach. Her voice, then, will be the most recognizable to her newborn infant.

The mother most likely will be her child's primary caretaker in times of illness, problems, and initial stages of development. Recognizing this reality doesn't negate the father's role. It simply allows the mother to take ownership of her significance in the child's life.

Intentional mothers understand that their purpose in being confident is to create an atmosphere of value and love for their children.

Your self-appreciation enhances your child's confidence in you and sets the tone for respect and trust, which strengthens and models a healthy example of self-worth.

I distinctly recall the day my mother interviewed for the position of school principal. She'd been an educator for many years and an assistant principal for five. I was curious about her interview process and experience. I asked Mom about the types of questions she was asked during the interview. I was most fascinated by the committee's last question and even more awed by my mother's response.

"Why should we hire you for the position of principal?" the chairman of the committee asked my mother.

"I should be hired for this position because I am qualified to do the job and do it well. I genuinely care about children and I believe that all children can learn. It will be my job to see to it that they're given every opportunity to do so," my mother declared in her feminine yet confident manner.

This moment in my mother's life was powerful to me as a daughter. It gave me a glimpse of healthy confidence and it came from the woman I most admired. I asked about her response and I still love her answer: "Cathy, if they are going to have confidence in me, they must see that I have it in myself. Why would they want to hire someone who doesn't believe she can do the job?"

The committee must have believed her because she and one other person were hired from among twelve highly qualified individuals. There was not, nor has there ever been, an arrogant bone in my mother's body; quiet, gentle confidence flows through her. This self-assurance flowed through her as a mother as well. The secret to my mother's self-worth was that she took her cues from God. She believed God loved her. He was her confidence. She really trusted Him to be what she needed and she trusted Him with us.

Throughout the course of my journey with my mother, I drew from her confidence.

It wasn't that she was perfect or always had an answer. We experienced many tragedies and losses over the course of my childhood, which impacted us greatly. Yet no matter how painful and unexpected life became, I always sensed that things would be okay. I believed it because my mother understood the importance of communicating an attitude of hope and faith in Christ regardless of circumstances. She knew that our view of the world was dependent on what she believed and how she interpreted life. She valued herself, understood how important she was to our sense of security, and knew our future confidence was dependent upon hers.

She knew her value.

She knew we needed to know ours.

She knew the two were related!

If you struggle with the issue of value in your life, here is where you begin your most important work. Your children are dependent on you making yourself a priority and embracing the value God has placed upon you. *Self-worth is caught, not taught.* Your children will learn to value themselves if they see you placing importance on recognizing your own value.

In contrast, if you take this issue lightly, the consequences to both you and your children will be costly. If you maintain your purpose as well as your self-worth, your children's self-confidence will be deep and sustainable.

Know Your Issues

When a mother is intent on raising secure, emotionally healthy children, she will set her mind on several important factors. These are issues that can trip us up and consequently spill over into our children's lives, becoming their issues too. We must first recognize the areas that trip us up and then find ways to overcome them. As our children watch us regain healthy attitudes and responses, this too will spill over into their lives and teach them to grow in healthier ways.

Develop Healthy Confidence

Here is a question to ponder: Has it ever dawned on you that your children are proud of you? Do your children know you're proud to be their mother? Remember: Being intentional means being *sharply focused*. How do you communicate to them your gratitude at the privilege of being their mom?

Children know on a variety of levels whether or not you're glad to have them as children. We may be able to fool a lot of people most of the time but we can't fool our children for long. They're born with sensors, and when a mother's heart struggles to "like" her child, something within that child knows. Most importantly, because children don't possess higher levels of thinking until they are older, their little minds immediately assume something is wrong with them. The result of this undeveloped thinking will be feelings of insecurity.

One day in one of our mother's groups, a woman was discussing her frustration with her son. She worked in the corporate world at a renowned company. "I've had attorneys and accountants answering to me throughout my career," she remarked, "but I can't get my two-year-old to listen to a thing I say!" In essence, she was telling me, "Sometimes I don't even like my child. Is this normal?"

In actuality, this mom's problem was not whether she liked her child. Her problem was a sense of inadequacy, because all the tricks she had in her diaper bag no longer worked.

Welcome to motherhood! She was just beginning to learn what confidence looks like from a mother's perspective.

Sometimes intentional motherhood is more than what you're *feeling*. It's spelled C-O-M-M-I-T-M-E-N-T—commitment. The determination to be the right type of mother for your child is more important than what you feel about your child at any given moment.

At times, every mother dislikes certain behaviors or attitudes her children demonstrate, but that is quite different from not liking your child. The truth about mothers struggling to like their children is that it usually has nothing to do with the child and everything to do with Mom feeling inadequate.

In such situations, two unfortunate things happen: First, the mother judges her value to the child based upon her own feelings of inadequacy. Second, the child interprets the mother's words of dislike as rejection, and she is the one the child longs to please. Intentional mothers recognize that children are responders and don't demand perfection. We can see this in two ways:

First, secure children know in their head as well as their heart that their mothers love them in spite of the way they behave. This doesn't imply that mothers should look away when their children disobey or act out. What it does say is that children know in their hearts that a mother's love is bigger than their own mistakes.

Second, a mother who focuses on communicating a sense of gratitude and confidence about being her child's mom uses words that acknowledge her appreciation. Have you ever said to your child, "I am so glad God chose me to be your mom"? This comment sends a powerful statement to your child that he or she is really special. While it may not completely register when they are little, it will have increasing impact as they get older.

Over the years, I frequently told my children that one of the ways I knew God loved me so much was by letting me be their mother. My children are in their early twenties as I write this, and to this day I let them know how grateful I am to have them in my life. The truth is, I truly believe I owe my children so much because they've been major catalysts for the most significant lessons in my life.

Another way to maintain a laser focus on communicating honor and pride to our children is to recognize that they're proud of us until given reason not to be. Their precious acceptance of us is a gift—one we should cherish and take as seriously as if it were coming from the most important adult in our lives.

I remember one day when I was a little girl, my mom was driving me to school. Mom always took pride in her appearance, and on this particular day I told her she looked pretty. Forty years later, I remember what she said to me as if it were yesterday.

"I always want you to be proud of me, Cathy!"

The idea that my opinion mattered to her stood out in my mind. The fact that she cared about my feelings made me feel ten feet tall. It never dawned on me until then that what I thought had so much value to her. From that time on, I looked at my mom, and myself, differently. I learned a lesson that stuck with me forever because Mom took the time to tell me that my thoughts and feelings mattered.

Being intentional by communicating your worth and their value to them allows you to pour the foundation on which confidence, character, and faith are built. Why is this so important?

It's called *integrity*.

Model Emotional Maturity

Raising children who are confident in whom God created them to be comes from mothers who are intentional about living a healthy identity first.

As the mother goes, so go the children. This one hurts, ladies!

It's one thing for us to tell our children that God created them in a marvelous and amazing image of Him. But if they hear us criticize ourselves, complain about our looks, and refer to ourselves in a derogatory manner, they won't believe what we say about God. They will live out our actions and deeds instead of our desires and words.

One night I dined at a Japanese restaurant and was seated at a hibachi table with a family I didn't know. As the meal progressed, we began polite conversation. Upon learning that I was a psychotherapist, the woman began to share some concerns she had about her five-year-old niece.

"The other day I took my daughter and niece to get some ice cream. My niece told me she couldn't have any, and when I inquired as to why, she told me that it had too many fat grams and would make her thighs get fat. Should I be concerned?" asked the aunt.

I told her, "I think you need to encourage your sister to get help as soon as possible."

I explained that if this child's mother didn't get a handle on her own issues, this little girl's chances of having an eating disorder were high. I went on to explain that for a five-year-old to be consumed with her appearance instead of the healthy interests associated with her age was dangerous. This mother and child needed intervention as soon as possible.

This experience brought home once again the truth that our actions are more powerful than our words. This little girl obviously had seen and heard her mother's obsession with her own size and weight. Regardless of what the mother may have said, it had already infiltrated the child's definition of self.

Can you say "wake-up call"?

As mothers we must be willing to seriously look at this area of our lives in order to live as an example to our children. Whatever insecurities exist in our hearts aren't meant to be covered up; they must be exposed for God to heal. If the shoe were on the other foot, wouldn't a mother encourage her child to deal with his or her self-image problem so as not to carry this baggage the rest of his or her life?

Absolutely!

Let's be honest. We don't want our children to be burdened with problems, shame, and inadequacies about themselves. But if our children are dealing with such issues, these problems could be originating from us. We must be willing to examine ourselves first. We can't expect something for our children that we won't do ourselves.

One of the blessings of being a mother is that God uses children to make us grow. Sometimes we may only feel as if we're a quarter of an inch ahead of them, but that is fine. It all boils down to a simple question: Am I going to live as an example of what God desires, or am I simply going to tell them to do as I say, not as I do?

Embrace Spiritual Maturity

Intentional mothers know that emotionally confident children aren't born but developed.

They recognize that a child who is internally confident, peaceful, and secure springs from a mother who sees herself from God's perspective. A woman who defines herself by the characteristics God has placed within her and not the way the world or her family of origin defines her. Intentional moms set their eyes on what is true and teach that truth throughout the course of their children's lives.

For several years, Neil and I experienced infertility. During many dark days in our home we faced a future without the possibility of children. After time and prayer, we believed God wanted us to adopt. We visited with an attorney, and within three months we had a precious little boy.

We anxiously awaited his arrival. Fortunately for us, my personal physician delivered him. Within an hour of all the papers being signed by the birth parents, my doctor brought our son to us. As we held him, we were in awe that we'd been given this precious gift.

Sitting alone in the hospital room holding Taylor, I began to tell this tiny little boy who he was going to be:

I told him he would grow up to be a kind, gentle man who would love God.

I told him he would have a wonderful sense of humor and would deeply love his family.

I assured him he would be wise, friendly, loving, and patient.

I told him I believed that with God's help, he could do anything he wanted.

Those little eyes stared back at me, as if soaking in every word I was saying. Over the years, I repeated that blessing to Taylor, even when he didn't have a clue what it all meant. For some reason, which I believe came from God, I felt it important that my son know immediately who he was and where he was going. I am happy to say that I see many of those characteristics in him today, while some are still unfolding. I believe God started the process the first day we held him.

Maybe you didn't grow up hearing your parents declare your value in a loving and positive way. Like many adults who grew up in nonverbal or dysfunctional families, you may have experienced injury to your self-worth, growing up with doubts and insecurities. The good news is that you don't have to hold on to that definition. You have the opportunity to let go of the past and begin to embrace a new definition of yourself from God's perspective. His opinion lasts for all eternity, while the opinion of man lasts only as long as you give it power to define you.

By understanding how important your own self-definition is to your children's self-worth, and then being intentional about yourself, you automatically give your children a head start in their journey to knowing themselves from God's perspective. Even more amazing is the observation I've gathered in years as a psychotherapist:

When a mother gives her children something she didn't receive as a child herself, God heals her heart in the process.

Know What You Want

This point may seem obvious, but let's try it out.

What do you want your children to look like when they're grown? I don't mean physically, but emotionally, spiritually, and mentally. Take a moment and jot down five or six characteristics you want to see manifested in your children by the time they are adults. You can be broad in your desires or specific.

Now look at your list. Is *honest* on there? How about *compassionate*? Did you mention you wanted a good *decision maker*?

You could list a hundred or so characteristics you might want your children to possess. All would probably be worthy attributes in developing an emotionally healthy person. But here are some questions to consider:

- How do you think your children will develop these virtues you cherish?

- By what method do you believe such values will become a part of the fabric of your child's character?

- When will you begin the process of instilling these beliefs and values?

Your purpose will be fulfilled when you can answer these questions with confidence and direction.

Intentional mothers know who they want their children to be as people, and therefore they set out on a course to make it happen.

On your journey, don't take things for granted or assume you'll have plenty of time to tackle it later. Recognize that it will take an entire childhood and adolescence to instill the things that really matter.

This process is called parenting.

More specifically—*motherhood.*

Being intentional as a mother involves a constant call to action. It's not enough to want your children to encompass godly virtues and values; you must be willing to model, teach, lead, and nurture them in the daily experiences called life. You will be asked to think in layers and create an atmosphere in your home conducive for your children to thrive and flourish from the inside out.

When our children were little, Neil and I were keenly aware of several attitudes we did *not* want manifested in our children. One of those attitudes was a sense of entitlement.

We didn't want our children growing up believing the world owed them something. We also didn't want Taylor and Tiffany thinking themselves superior to others. We wanted our children to have servant hearts and a strong work ethic. We wanted them to possess a grateful spirit that was humble and generous.

We knew that for them to capture these values, all of which were biblical in their foundation, we needed to see these characteristics as a thread to be woven in the things we did, lived, and taught every day.

Over the years, this value took on many forms and faces. We took them to nursing homes to see elderly people who were often alone. They participated in serving holiday dinners for the indigent as well as Christmas parties for homeless children. They participated in the deaf ministry and learned sign language. From early childhood to their senior year of high-school, investing in others was a way of life.

We also interwove delayed gratification into their lives. We believed it was important to teach them how to wait graciously. God doesn't always answer every request immediately, and neither did we.

Can I tell you how grateful I am that we thought this through?

I wish I could tell you that Neil and I thought through every value we embrace, but we didn't. However, the ones with which we were intentional have paid off in our children's lives.

Being intentional about your child's life means you must develop a definition of *healthy and successful*. Asking God to give you that definition is like going on a road trip and picturing your final destination. You begin to paint an image in your mind and heart as to what God had in mind when He created your children. As these precious gifts unfold in front of you, God will continue to direct your path and your vision for who they are. Your confidence in that vision will be contagious to your children, and they will cling to your definition of success until they possess confidence of their own.

Most importantly, God will be intentional with you as you develop your intentional picture of your children. Though you encounter adventure and surprises along the way, you also will arrive at the destination born in your heart. When all is said and done, you can handle anything you and your child or teen might encounter when your heart is in line with God throughout your child's journey.

FAITH POINTS

. . . who has saved us and called us to a holy life—
not because of anything we have done but because of
his own purpose and grace. This grace was given us
in Christ Jesus before the beginning of time.

~ 2 Timothy 1:9 ~

When we follow Christ, His purpose becomes our purpose. He says in this verse that it is not to be the result of our work but of His work through us. For mothers to raise healthy children, we must stay focused on God's purpose for us: to be *intentional* in loving our children the way Christ loves us.

1. Have you ever considered whether you are mothering your children *intentionally*? If so, how? If not, why not?

2. What is your purpose as a mother? Write down the outcomes you envision for your children when they become adults.

3. Do you think this purpose will or should change as your children grow older?

4. Which issue of motherhood do you need to work on the most—healthy confidence, emotional maturity, or spiritual maturity—and how can you grow in that area?

5. What was the greatest insight you gained from this chapter, and how can you put it to use today?

WHY GOOD KIDS
DON'T FEEL GOOD

Principle 2: Be Intentional about Knowing Your Child

I once knew a precious little girl. She had a gentle spirit, a loving heart, and twinkling eyes. She possessed an innocence that was sweet, though a little flighty. My family loved Carly the moment we met her.

Carly had an amazing smile and loved to be loved. She was affectionate, polite, and always willing to be helpful, wanting to please others. Despite this, by the time our family met her when she was ten, she seemed to make herself somewhat invisible with other people, as if she didn't want to be seen. She had trouble looking you in the eyes, and yet you could see that she wanted to connect with you. We saw her sweet, unique nature and accepted Carly for who she was. The more she got to know us, the more she responded. With our family, she was not hesitant. Her natural self came out when she felt accepted, though she was still withdrawn.

The challenge for Carly was her mother. A dear and wonderful woman in her own right, Carly's mom, Charlotte, just didn't understand her.

She didn't "know" her daughter.

She kept trying to put Carly in a particular box drawn by Charlotte's own expectations and assumptions, and Carly just wouldn't fit into it. During Carly's childhood and adolescent years, Charlotte genuinely believed that Carly was being difficult. Charlotte didn't realize the underlying problem wasn't her daughter; it was her own failure to grasp and comprehend who her daughter truly was.

As a result of this misunderstanding early in her life, young adulthood for Carly has been a rough road. She is still the precious girl I knew her to be, but she's made choices that have hurt her—and those around her—deeply, all because, I believe, she simply wasn't "known."

Carly was a "good kid" who wasn't allowed to be the person she was created to be.

How often have you heard someone say, "He's such a good kid," or "That family is blessed to have such good kids"? Yet what exactly is a "good kid"? How do you define one? How do you know one when you see one?

Most moms think their kids fall into that category, but they still might have difficulty defining a "good kid." In fact, many mothers find it easier to tell you the opposite, what good kids "don't do" or what bad kids look like. They might say, "Well, good kids don't . . ." Defining kids with negative behaviors speaks volumes about what most of us notice.

On the other hand, good kids often go unnoticed and unappreciated. Moms with such children are grateful for routine behavior, yet they communicate their displeasure when the status quo is interrupted. Good kids tend to comply with the rules, have a cooperative spirit, and are the pride of their parents.

Unfortunately, many of these good kids don't feel "good." I'm not talking about physical health but emotional and spiritual health. Sometimes these children don't possess the confidence one would think is displayed in a good kid.

Instead, they're uncertain and feel inadequate. They might act nice, but the core of their soul questions whether they are good. These kids know Mom and Dad are pleased when they are cooperative, but often their parents don't communicate to these children a sense of great value or unconditional love. If as a mom you equate your child's compliance with self-confidence, you will be sadly disappointed.

More importantly, you will lose valuable time instilling your child's worth and value.

How?

You aren't instilling worth and value; instead, you're assuming it's already present.

Sometimes we mothers assume that our children's compliance means they have positive self-worth. After all, they don't question us. They obey us; they don't cause trouble. They must feel good about themselves, right?

Not necessarily.

They could be responding out of anxiety, fear of rejection, or need.

The more time you spend living with this false assumption, the more your children will experience a greater sense of emptiness regarding their own value. If you don't catch it in time, it will take a crisis to discover that your kid isn't okay; that he or she struggles with self-worth.

So what is the problem?

> Where do things go wrong?

>> How do good kids fail to attain a sense of value when they "do all the right things"?

It's easy. It happens when mothers have the wrong definition of "good" and fail to *know* their children.

To be honest, this wasn't God's intention. He had a different plan. He created mothers to be the experts on their children.

You.

Not other professionals. Not other family members.

You! You're *the* expert!

Nobody knows a child like his mother.

Now I recognize that you may feel inadequate, overwhelmed, and ill equipped. However, put your feelings aside and let's look at the facts: No one knows your child better than you do.

You know when something is wrong.

You know when they just need a hug.

You know when they need you to be their advocate.

God created you to be the one with whom your child entered the world. Children come from the womb of a woman, whether adopted or born to you. We were designed to carry, nurture, feed, and connect with our children. We were given responsibility for their care and safety. We were wired to "know" them.

GET TO "KNOW" YOUR CHILDREN

I know it sounds rather odd to say that moms need to know their children. You're probably thinking that I'm stating the obvious because, of course, all mothers know their children. But I don't mean "knowing" in the context of *recognition*. I am talking about *comprehending* your children.

Knowing your children necessitates more than simply living in the same house with them. It is more than routinely doing all the things mothers do. Knowing requires us to be intentional in understanding our children—including their individual personalities and character.

When we know our kids, we recognize their vulnerabilities and weaknesses. We give ourselves permission to see what is actually there, not simply what we want to see. We can anticipate their responses to stress, disappointment, and hurt. We recognize whether they are shy or outgoing and don't force them to become something God did not wire them to be.

When a mother doesn't know her child the way the child needs her to, they both suffer.

Let me explain.

I once had a friend whose son was a typical little boy, and his mother was nurturing but strict. She had four other children who were well-behaved and obedient, so she was confident that her parenting style was appropriate.

The only problem was, her youngest son wasn't getting with her program.

Over and over again, this mother consistently followed through in her discipline, yet still her youngest son appeared to ignore his parents' instructions. He was always in trouble, living perpetually in the corner or getting spanked. His mother was truly perplexed, frustrated, and worried.

On the verge of losing it, the mother began seeking the input of friends and professionals. When the boy was almost three, his mother discovered that her son was hearing-impaired and needed hearing aids to function normally.

While this mother was relieved that she finally knew what was wrong with her son, she experienced tremendous guilt over all the times she punished him for things he didn't understand. She struggled for a long time before she could forgive herself.

Were there clues that this child was deaf before the age of three?

Probably.

Yet this mother is a typical example of a well-meaning mom raising four other children, heavily involved in her family and activities. Her problem was that she could not step outside her frame of reference to see other possibilities. She got stuck looking at her child from a specific, preconceived behavioral perspective, which prohibited her from seeing the clues that were present.

STUDY YOUR KIDS

For you and me to fully comprehend the depth of our child's personality, spirit, and unique wiring, we need to become students of that child:

To look upon him as a book to be read, studied, and investigated.

To view her with wonder and anticipation of discovery.

To step outside our box and see what is, not what we want to see.

When a mother learns from her child, she has greater confidence in knowing his needs, grasping the way he processes and learns, and seeing his vulnerabilities. She learns to understand the way her child expresses and receives love; she learns to understand his quirks and fears. She doesn't allow her own biases to get in the way, and she remains teachable in her attitude.

A "student" mom recognizes that each child is born with individual differences, and some with more difficult issues than others.

Some children enter the world very defined. They're strong-willed in the beginning and attempt to command the household early on.

They're often the most vocal, demanding, and determined. They constantly challenge us (as well as any other adult in charge) and push us quickly to our limit.

Other children are difficult because they have issues that aren't easily, if ever, fixed. Children with learning issues, emotional disorders, and birth defects bring a new level of stress to a mother's heart. These challenges bring additional learning opportunities we never anticipated.

Can you see how becoming a "student" of your children is necessary in such situations?

An intentional mother doesn't fight the differences or difficulties.

She recognizes that God had something in mind when He gave her each child. She trusts that God wants to show her something through her relationship with her "challenge" child that she would not have learned in any other capacity. And she learns to apply her knowledge to each child, even those who appear to be easier than the others.

Intentional mothers also recognize that while an "easy" child may demand less emotional energy to parent, easy children have their own unique set of needs that deserve priority attention. Failure to do so can result in dependent, insecure children and teens.

Easy children can't be taken for granted, underestimated, or ignored, because they're no less deep in potential, possibilities, or intellectual capacity.

I once knew a family of four children who had one child that was more compliant than the other three. This son quickly learned that it was best to stay off his mother's radar screen because bad things resulted whenever her children were the center of her focus.

This boy grew up passive, having mostly escaped the dysfunction of the family because he learned to become invisible by being easy and compliant. While this method of coping was remarkable for a child, the damage was still there and followed him into adulthood. Fortunately for this child, when he became a man, he found a wife who appreciated him and challenged him to find his voice and be emotionally visible. She welcomed all dimensions of who he was. This "easy" child paid a big price as an adult because his gentleness was not appreciated, respected, or developed early on.

No matter what type of child you have—easy, challenging, difficult—your job as a mom is to *know* each individual child you raise by studying your kids.

Having the mind-set of a student allows you to get the most out of every motherhood experience. It opens your heart, mind, and spirit to see things you might not otherwise. The framework of "studying" and "knowing" your child provides multiple layers and levels with which to filter your child's life.

Learn to be a student; it keeps your focus on your child and not yourself.

Did you catch that last line?

Allow the difficulties of motherhood to become a pathway to knowing your child better, and you will learn a lot about yourself in the process. But the focus must stay on the *child*, because if your child's challenges become more about you than your child, your child loses.

Here is an oxymoron of motherhood:

> Focusing on your child will teach you about yourself.

> Focusing on yourself will deprive you of knowing your child.

Isn't that profound?

And isn't that just like God?

When we invest in our children with a teachable mind, we become wiser on every level. When we step outside the box of limitations to see the possibilities, our children gain greater confidence. When we are intentional mothers, deeper levels of trust, respect, and love develop between our children and us.

Sandpaper and Puzzles

At this moment you may be feeling as if you're a thousand miles away from fitting the definition of an intentional mother. Maybe you think your children bring out the worst in you. Maybe you feel the most inadequate in the relationships you love the most.

If so, you're headed in the right direction.

In fact, you have never been closer to where you need to be.

Because here is the secret:

Children are the sandpaper God uses to refine our rough edges.

We often think we are given children so we can impact the world through them. Our dream is to teach and lead them, and thereby make a difference with our wisdom, experience, and love. There's an element of truth in such thinking.

But here is another thought:

Maybe God gave you kids to teach you dependence on Him.

How about humility?

Or perseverance?

Is God trying to teach you any of these qualities through your parenting?

The arena of motherhood exposes the opportunities to recognize and develop these characteristics. We aren't typically born with these virtues; instead they develop through life experiences. And who are our teachers? Our children.

Some children are compliant and easygoing, which sends a certain signal to a mom: "Hey, I'm going to be easy and wonderful to parent!" As a mother of these "easier" children, your confidence remains high. It is difficult to believe that the wheels could fall off the cart when your child is such a pleasure to parent.

Or so you may think.

I recently met with a seventeen-year-old daughter and her mother because the daughter began lying to her parents about a multitude of issues. Her unacceptable behavior only manifested itself the past few months.

As I explored this young woman's history, her mom revealed she'd been compliant, gentle, quiet, and obedient most of her life. However, one tiny red flag stuck out: the daughter was sneaky. As a youngster, she would do "little" things—like steal cookies and sneak out of her room at nap time to go downstairs and watch TV. While not a huge issue at the time, this and other minor incidents may have been a precursor to her current behavior.

And she is an "easy" child.

So let's get down to an important truth:

Children are a puzzle.

At any point in time they can present an opportunity for us to grow. They may make a sudden U-turn or take us for a wild ride, and immediately we feel blindsided because we didn't put the pieces together.

Our kids are complex. We underestimate them when they are little and seem less complicated and less dimensional. Underestimating a child creates a hole in his heart, an emotional wound that never heals. The damaging result is that he will never truly believe in himself.

Suddenly our children grow older, and we're surprised when they become opinionated, difficult, and unpredictable. Yet all of these characteristics fall within the definition of normal development.

Children spend their lives unfolding, although some stages of their lives reveal more than others. Our kids don't plan to be complex, but they do depend upon those closest to them to interpret their changing nuances.

Intentional mothers know that one of their primary roles is to translate to their children who each child is, and is becoming.

To do this well, we must constantly observe our kids, clarify what we see, and communicate this knowledge to help our kids better understand themselves. We are the dot connectors between the pieces of our children's heart, soul, mind, and body.

Connect the dots.

It sounds so simple.

It is anything but.

Connecting your children's pieces helps them discover who they are, what they need, how they think, and where they are headed. It will take time, insight, patience, and perseverance. This role lasts your entire lifetime, though how you connect the pieces changes as children move through adolescence and into adulthood.

Over the years, I've discovered that any mother with more than one child has one they seem to grasp with greater ease than the others. She doesn't love the easy child any greater; however, the child she doesn't "get" as easily forces her to grow in ways she never planned or expected.

With her more difficult child, she recognizes she will not live in her comfort zone, and this realization already makes her a better mother. By admitting that things won't be business as usual, a mom greatly improves her ability to read the cues of her child's individuality. While this may be stressful from one perspective, it is exciting and welcoming from another.

While our "challenging" children are an obvious puzzle, perhaps the greater danger is to assume the "easy" or more predictable child has let you in on all the secrets of his or her mind and heart. This isn't a safe belief; embracing it will come back to haunt you later, at a more vulnerable age in your child's life. The challenge here is to not become complacent in parenting easy children. We must recognize that they can surprise us, and it's just as important to "know" them well.

No matter whether your child is easy or difficult, you need to see the challenges and benefits in both.

Like many mothers, I had one of each.

My son was high maintenance, though he had no idea how exhausting he could be. My daughter was so compliant she could become invisible in a home with such a challenging brother. I love both my children more than life itself, yet clearly they needed different things from me as a mom.

In my early years of parenting Taylor, it became obvious that God gave me the privilege to mother a little boy who wouldn't walk to the tune of a common drummer.

Taylor always thought on a different level and asked a lot of questions.

He never rushed or hurried.

While very intelligent, as a child he struggled with common sense.

To really appreciate the unique way God wired Taylor, someone had to take the time to really *know* him. Once they did so, people really liked him and appreciated the depth of his heart and soul. This boy became a tender young man who is gentle, loving, and kind.

And he's still unique.

While obviously I needed to be on top of my game with Taylor, Tiffany's needs were less noticeable. Fortunately, God had a plan to clue me in about my children. For me, it was homeschooling.

I began homeschooling each of my children when they were in the third grade and continued for their fourth and fifth grades. I balanced my career with their educational needs during most of those years. We had a great support system and many wonderful people in their lives, but what they needed most was me—especially Tiffany. I stayed home full-time for Tiffany's last year of homeschooling and Taylor's first year in middle school.

Can I tell you how grateful I am?

What I learned about Tiffany during that year at home laid a foundation for the years ahead. It was a year of emotional restoration for her because she had me all to herself. She traveled with me to my speaking engagements, and I created learning experiences out of everything we did. She had the opportunity to soak me up and connect with me on a deep level, which increased her self-confidence and her willingness to try new things.

Our intense time together allowed me to learn her depth, experience the breadth of her intelligence, and appreciate her amazing heart. All these things I had observed on some level, but not to the degree I needed to know.

As I became a student of my daughter, I learned that much healing took place when we touched. I'd seen glimpses of this when we first began homeschooling, because Tiffany came to me for a hug between each subject we studied. My daughter was always affectionate, but this physical touch dynamic taught me a critical lesson. As I began to grasp the significance of touch for her, I decided to create a way to meet the deeper layers of her heart.

Whenever Tiffany hugged me, it would be up to her to let go first.

Regardless of how long a hug lasted, I held her until she released. At times our hugs lasted a long while. I often had no idea what she was feeling that warranted such a lengthy connection.

One hug that particularly stood out in my heart lasted more than fifteen minutes, standing in our kitchen.

No words were spoken between us.

Just a child drawing from the emotional well of her mother's heart when she needed it most.

Tiffany also learned that I didn't need her to justify any hug. I simply accepted them with silent understanding between us. To this day, our "hug" rule still applies.

This physical exchange accomplished several things. First of all, my daughter knew I understood she had needs that words might not help. Second, it taught her responsibility for getting her needs met. Third, it communicated to her that I comprehended her on a deep level. Fourth, it showed her that I was never in too big a hurry or too distracted to give her my time and attention.

This example is one of many ways God revealed to me who my children are and what I need to know to communicate my acceptance of them. This information is paramount if moms want their children to learn who they are as people in this world. Let me explain.

FROM STUDENT TO TEACHER

The father's voice has a resounding impact upon children and his words linger with them forever. His praise and criticism record in their minds and play back in critical moments of their need. The father's influence is dramatic and can't be diminished.

Yet the mother's voice is the most prevalent voice heard by a child. Our role in our children's identity surfaces quickly in the formation of our child's self-worth. We are the primary nurturers in the first few months.

If we breast-feed our child, our voice continually resonates in his ears and heart.

If we've adopted our child, we intentionally saturate him with our presence.

As our children grow and we begin to comprehend them, we communicate back to them knowledge about who they are. Herein lies the heart behind a mother being a student of her children.

Intentional mothers have the privilege of taking the knowledge, information, and insight about their children and feeding it back to them so they can begin to formulate a definition of themselves.

In other words, the better student of your child you become, the better teacher you will be as you communicate your children's personality, character, and purpose back to them. Some call this process "encouragement," a word derived from the French words *en* (to put in) and *coeur* (heart): to put into the heart.

Communicating your child's traits to him or her is one of the most important jobs you will ever conduct during your motherhood journey. Your knowledge of them communicated back to them helps your children develop a sense of value, awareness of their gifts and talents, and insight into their values and beliefs.

I once knew a woman who struggled with self-worth. She'd recently moved from California, and she attended one of our motherhood seminars. In the process she realized she did not want to pass down to her children the issues she wrestled with. Her story was powerful.

One of several children, Hannah grew up in a home with an extremely critical mother. Her father wasn't emotionally present and seldom let his interest or concern for her be known. She figured out early on that she was intelligent and could do well in school. In fact, the only positive attention Hannah ever received was in the classroom.

Because she was so smart, she bored easily, so she talked to the other students during class. Her report card—straight As—usually also included a comment about Hannah talking too much in class. Every time she handed her perfect report card to her mom, the mother would say, "Any fool can keep their mouth shut!"

How is that for communicating love and acceptance?

During her senior year in high-school, Hannah began her college application submissions, knowing that her family had little to contribute to her education. Her mother made it very clear that she needed to stay close to home and told her daughter, "No one will want you anyway." Hannah begged her mother for the $35 application fee for Yale University, but the mother refused because she knew Yale wouldn't want her daughter.

On the last possible day, Hannah's mother relented and gave her daughter the money to accompany her application. Months passed by, and finally the day arrived—Hannah's letter from Yale came in the mail. Not only was she accepted but she also received a full-ride scholarship!

After Hannah graduated from Yale, she entered the work world successfully. But a degree from the world's most prestigious uni-

versity still didn't erase the doubt, criticism, and emotional neglect from her mother.

Hannah wanted to heal from the inside out.

She knew she was damaged and that it was unacceptable to stay
that way. She faced the tough task of reprogramming her mind
to change the messages—in her mother's voice—that lingered in
her head. God's voice needed to replace her mom's critical voice.
After all, He, not her mother, was the one who most accurately
defined her.

*Intentional mothers understand the challenge before them. They rec-
ognize that the most confident children and teens are those who learn
that their value isn't in what they've accomplished, how well they
obey, or how hard they've worked. Intentional mothers realize that
for their offspring to arrive at young adulthood with the healthy self-
worth God intended, they need to comprehend they have value simply
because they are.*

During my motherhood conferences, I often ask mothers to reflect on several key thoughts. I begin by asking them to remember
back to when their children were eighteen months old. This is a
cute age where toddlers have developed enough individual personality that their mothers see a glimpse of what is coming down
the pike. Yet they're still dependent on their parents for their well-
being. They're still in diapers and have to be dressed, have their
food prepared for them, and need to be protected from danger.
They can't do anything for anyone or much for themselves.

When mothers at my conferences capture this memory of that
young child in their minds, smiles break out on their faces. They
report feeling joy, hope, and overwhelming love when they freeze-
frame that image in their mind.

I then ask them to focus on the current image of their children.

I give them a minute to remember their older faces.

Then I ask them to recall the last time they broke into a smile simply because their children existed. Maternal smiles slowly dissipate as these moms realize something is interfering in their level of acceptance and value of their children. This is a sobering moment for most mothers because it demonstrates the ease with which we can lose sight of the value of our own flesh and blood.

When a mother's passion dwindles, children—especially teens and young adults—quickly sense it. They've lived with her long enough to feel her frustration and disappointment long before she even recognizes it. This struggle is a statement about the mother's faith. She really is grappling with God, not her children, which brings this journey full circle.

All mothers have moments when they feel discouraged, over-whelmed, fearful, or angry.

Intentional mothers, however, allow such moments to remind them of this truth: *God does not make mistakes, and nothing in their lives or their children's lives will ever surprise God.*

Remember that God is your biggest fan and He never gives up on you.

Or your children.

So What's the Problem?

You and I need to remind our children often about God's definition of them. Let them know that God loves them in spite of their behavior, not because of it. God's love is unconditional whether we "act" good or bad. We moms must remind our kids that no one in the world is like them, and that we are constantly amazed God chose us to be their mother. When we consistently reinforce the truth that God is our kid's biggest fan, they will see Him for who He really is, not how He often is portrayed by religion and the world. And they'll begin to learn how to see themselves through God's eyes.

Sometimes we also may need to remind ourselves about God's love for *us*. He is the final authority on who our children are, how they were created, where they are headed, and how they will get there. At times we will feel inadequate for the parenting task, but in our weaknesses, we can see God's strength—both in our lives and our children's.

Let's get real about this thought for a minute.

I want to use a religious word with you.

Grace.

You may know what this word means.

If not, I hope you will understand that most Christians think they "get" this definition, but don't.

How do I know that?

Because I know what goes on behind the scenes with most Christian kids, and they would rather die than let their parents know their secrets, problems, or difficulties. And these are kids from families who think they understand grace. In actuality, these moms (and dads) don't have a clue what grace looks like in their parenting, or for that matter, in themselves.

Grace is a concept that means, "I am going to love you whether you deserve it or not."

Grace means, "You don't have to earn my love."

Grace means, "No matter what you do, I will always be your biggest fan."

In contrast to grace, most good kids believe they are loved conditionally. They think they are loved because they make their parents happy. Happy by:

- being a good student.

- getting into the "right" school.

- being a leader.

- doing well in a sport or creative endeavor.

- living a moral life.

But what if something goes wrong? Crisis.

- When grades fall, children question whether they are loved.

- When teens make goofy decisions, they're convinced their parents will never trust them again.

- When children—of any age—"disappoint" their parents, they're frightened of how it will cost their relationship with their parents.

This is why good kids don't necessarily feel good about themselves. They won't feel good if they perceive they are valued only by their behavior—if they're measured by what they *do*.

Sometimes mothers allow pride, selfishness, and other people's opinions to override what their children need most: unconditional love. A common mothering mistake I hear is, "What will other people think of me as a mother if my child misbehaves?" This mom is putting her own needs before her child's.

While you might never have thought such a thing, the reality is that you may be sending negative messages to your kids—even inadvertently—messages that say you do not accept them and their flaws.

Think about this. By the age of ten, kids have figured out how much their mothers can handle. They realize that if Mom "wigs out" over lost homework or broken curfew, they better not tell her something that really matters. They've listened to Mom's comments about other kids who make mistakes, and know they can expect the same reaction if they find themselves in a similar place.

What have your kids decided about how much you can handle?

What messages from you have registered with your kids that, as a result, are now impacting their self-confidence?

Most important, what have your children learned about God's acceptance of them from their relationship with you? (Remember: acceptance does not equal permissiveness.)

Intentional mothers know:

A child who knows he is loved simply because he exists is a child who most likely will feel good from the inside out.

> If a mom loves herself the way God loves her, she will raise children who experience unconditional love.

> > Mothers who recognize the power they have in their children's lives will make the world look different from the one in which we live now.

The purest love an intentional mother can have for her child is to know her child's weaknesses, flaws, struggles, and issues, and in knowing, love them with acceptance, anticipation, and hope—with God's grace. Are you learning to know your child? Do you love your child with that type of love?

❧❀❧

FAITH POINTS

O LORD, you have searched me
and you know me.
You know when I sit and when I rise;

you perceive my thoughts from afar.
You discern my going out and my lying down;
you are familiar with all my ways.
Before a word is on my tongue
you know it completely, O LORD.
You hem me in—behind and before;
you have laid your hand upon me.
Such knowledge is too wonderful for me,
too lofty for me to attain.

~ Psalm 139:1–6 ~

One of the exciting dimensions of the character of God is His thorough knowledge of each of His children. We are called to emulate that dimension of God with our own children. By knowing your kids well, you will have access to a deeper part of their heart because they will know your love is unconditional.

1. How well do you believe you know your children?

2. What have you learned from each of your children lately?

3. How can you be a better "student" of your children? How will doing so benefit them?

4. How can your children change you for the better, sanding your rough edges?

5. What was the greatest insight you gained from this chapter, and how can you put it to use today?

3

YOU CAN LIVE PEACEFULLY IN THE TEENAGE YEARS

Principle 3: Be Intentional about Being a Vision Keeper

Hal was in the seventh grade and one of the easiest kids in the world to get along with. He was having trouble with a teacher at school but he hadn't told his mom or dad. One morning, Hal decided he just couldn't handle the rejection at school anymore, so he took matters into his own hands.

Hal lived in a housing development in the middle of an orange grove. On this particular morning, he decided to use his natural environment to help his cause—he strategically stuck nails in some oranges and placed the oranges in the path of his school bus.

Yes, that's right.

Hal and all of the other kids did not get to school on time that morning. A school bus with nail-laden oranges clinging to its tires has difficulty reaching its final destination. The trick also landed my brother in a heap of trouble.

Was Hal a delinquent? No.

A lot of parents might have thought they had a troubled kid. Fortunately for Hal, our parents knew him and believed his act of desperation that morning was simply a single incident in his life, not a defining moment.

Hal was a *teenager*, and for some parents, the thought of adolescence creates enormous apprehension.

If you're dreading the teenage years, you're already in trouble. But remember, your parents lived through that season of life with you—and they survived. Now your kids deserve for you to live through it with them; it won't kill you either.

At least I don't think it will.

Your child's adolescence is a self-fulfilling prophecy:

> If you expect it to be exciting and interesting, it will.

> But if you expect it to be bad, you won't be disappointed.

> If you dread something long enough, it becomes as bad as you imagined.

Adolescence brings out a mother's greatest fears. Maybe she fears her children will act like she did during her adolescence. Or she's all too familiar with the incredible peer pressures our culture places on teens. Whatever the cause of her concerns, it permeates her belief about the adolescent age. Unfortunately, she doesn't hear enough encouragement to dissuade her anxious thoughts, nor does she see enough examples of hope. Left to her own mind, a mom can create a nightmare of expectation for the teen years before her child is out of diapers.

The saddest thing about her ongoing fear is that the child picks up on it, and the anxiety becomes a thread in the child's thinking as well. While both mother and child may unknowingly participate in this unconscious collusion, eventually it will surface in the fulfillment of their negative expectations.

Does that sound sick to you?

Perhaps. Yet there is an antidote—keeping the big picture in mind, keeping the vision about who you believe they can become.

This principle—being a vision keeper—begins by examining a mother's faulty thinking. Mothers must deeply reflect on what they expect to happen to their children in the teen years, and then ask themselves several key questions:

Are my thoughts out of fear?

Is my anxiety about me and my past?

Are my fears or expectations connected to what I hear from other mothers and the stories they tell?

I once met with a high-school senior and her mother in my counseling office. The girl was about to graduate and leave for college. Tension had escalated between the two because Mom was fearful that her daughter would make some poor choices after she moved away.

As the session unfolded, the girl said to her mom, "I am not you. I won't make the mistakes and choices you did. I don't need to do that. You needed to go through all of that for some reason. I don't need to go there. I don't want to do that to myself!"

This teenage girl succinctly drew the line that her mom's fears were about her mother's past and not about the daughter's current journey. The girl was hurt because her mother wasn't giving her the trust she deserved. Mom's fears were clearly wounding a previously healthy relationship.

Every kid deserves a clean slate on which to chart his or her own journey. If we're intentional in giving that to our children, they will know in their hearts we're treating them with trust and fairness. They also are assured that we will walk alongside them.

This "vision keeper" principle will challenge the way you view your children during this ever-so-important time in their lives. So sit back, take a breath, and listen to a heart-and-head message that will encourage and strengthen you from the inside out. This principle asks you to be intentional about your *attitude* toward your children during the teenage years. You can learn that any single adolescent event need not define your child's future when you keep the big picture uppermost in your mind.

DON'T LOSE THE VISION IN THE MOMENT

Face it. Most teens will make their share of stupid mistakes. Part of this phase of life development is discovering identity, and that process is not devoid of missteps. One of the most common errors mothers make during a child's adolescence is pronouncing doom over their teen's entire future when their teen acts in a stupid or irresponsible manner. Too often mothers treat a single offense as if it were permanently fatal, which few things in life are. These moments of youthful immaturity or impulsivity often create intense fear, anger, and over-the-top maternal reactions.

At this point, mothers allow their secret fears to become addictive, and they forget their major responsibility, which is to recognize the impact of a present moment while not forgetting that moment's future potential in their child's life.

Each situation you face with your child is bigger than the moment at hand. For instance, if you wig out over your son leaving his sneakers in the middle of the floor, he will conclude that you can't handle the real issues in his life in a safe and reasonable manner.

When this happens, you lose your intention and your trust relationship with your child.

If you define your children or teens by a moment in time or by a series of events, you tell them they are defined by *what they do* and not *who they are*. In an age that saturates our youth with superficial definitions of value, we must speak the voice of truth to our kids' hearts and minds. We cannot cave into the fear that they themselves feel when they mess up.

When you can begin to see this for your children, they can begin to believe it for themselves.

Many years ago, I worked with a young woman who, as a teenager, snuck out one Halloween night to go to a party. Her parents did not want her going because they did not know any of the kids or the families at this event. The daughter made her own decision.

Unfortunately for this girl, this night out became a nightmare.

While Sherry was at the party, a guy she'd just met raped her. Someone had slipped her a pill that made her so groggy it was impossible for her to fight him off. Horrified and scared by what happened to her, and frightened of telling her parents, Sherry kept the tragedy to herself.

Many months later, she discovered an outbreak she'd previously never had. Weeping, Sherry finally told her mother about the outbreak—and the rape.

In spite of the trauma of Sherry's situation, her mom did something right:

First, she didn't focus on the "why" of what happened. She focused on the need her daughter had—to feel safe, to be accepted, and to be taken care of. Her mom knew the "why" might or might not come later, but she kept her daughter's need at the forefront of the situation.

Her mother lovingly began the healing process with her daughter and helped her get the various types of support she needed, including coming to my office for counseling,

As I began to work with Sherry, she gradually revealed the thoughts behind her tears.

"My life will never be the same again. I will never trust a man again. I will always be damaged goods. I will never look at life the same way. I will never see myself the way I used to!"

A sense of sadness, remorse, and despair filled the room as she spoke.

But something even worse sat with us: *distorted thinking*.

I knew that while I needed to be sensitive to Sherry's feelings, I could not allow her to believe for one second longer that her life was over.

"Yes, your life has changed," I told her. "I am so sad that you experienced a very brutal and unkind wound to your body, mind, and heart. But let me say this. This one moment in life does not define you. Something awful happened to you, but it does not have the power to define you unless you let it."

I continued.

"Sherry, you will reach a place where you will live with confidence again. There will come a time when you are healed, so that even though you might have the memory of the experience, you won't have the pain anymore. You will heal, and you won't be defined by someone else's actions."

Sherry needed to hear a voice of authority speak confidently and boldly into her life about who she was and how she was defined.

All kids and most adults need to hear and believe that circumstances don't define us. We need to know that we're bigger than our life situations because that means our destiny and identity are not in someone else's hands.

A MIND UNDER SIEGE

Adolescence is a difficult time in development. According to scientists, the adolescent brain is under immense transition. Thus, in spite of our wondering at times just what our kids might be thinking, there are legitimate reasons as to why teens don't always make sound decisions.

For instance, did you know that neurological studies of adolescent brains show that teens:

- are impulsive.

- do not comprehend danger.

- cannot recognize the consequences of their actions.

- have difficulty prioritizing.

- misread emotional signals.

- have difficulty with organization.[1]

Teens not only have cognitive challenges but they also struggle with friendships, hormones, academics, and peer pressure. They question everything they've been taught and explore new things with curiosity and judgment. They don't know who they are and they wonder who we are. Adolescence is a time when they need us the most but are often too scared to admit it to themselves or us. We must be careful not to confuse this fear with stubbornness.

These are just a few indicators that make adolescence a complex time for both teens and parents. So instead of jumping to conclusions that we've failed or our kids are losers, we may need to step back, breathe, and remember that our kids are going through a difficult period in their lives.

From middle school to senior year, your child is experiencing turmoil, fear, and a strong sense of inadequacy. While this season may be noted for rebellion, impulsivity, and short-term thinking, mothers can't buy into that definition of a teenager. Instead, intentional moms become the keeper of the vision.

What vision are we talking about?

Remember when your kids were born? Whether adopted or biological, your children planted hopes and dreams in your heart—a vision for their lives that brought meaning and excitement to your life. You believed the best for them and imagined them to be the best at whatever they chose to do. You had a vision of them that was fresh, filled with hope and confidence.

Then things began to change.

Life didn't go the way you planned.

Maybe your children are different than you expected and have minds of their own. Or they've made bad choices, or hang out with the wrong type of friends. Perhaps they have learning disabilities or struggle with relationships, neither of which you were prepared for. Maybe you see too much of yourself or their dad in them and are sure that will slow them down. Slowly, without much fanfare or attention, the exciting vision you had for your children diminishes. It is so gradual that you don't realize it is happening until perhaps this very moment. You've lost the big picture; it got swallowed up in real life.

Crises show us—and our teens—our true opinion of them. In other words, if your vision for their future is still as meaningful as when they were born, they'll see that in you, even in the midst of difficult circumstances. Yet the opposite is also true: they'll notice if your vision for them is now tarnished.

It is easy to be at your best when things are going well and life is sweet. However, teens need you to be your best when they are at their worst. In those moments you must be the keeper of the vision God gave you when your teenager was a newborn baby.

Your job as a mom is critical to your teens in the challenging moments of life because they will look to you to see what you truly believe about them. They need to see confidence and hope when no one else sees it for them—perhaps not even themselves. Who will they look to first for that affirmation? You.

Children have enough opposition—teachers riding them about schoolwork, coaches yelling at them to get it right this time, friends deserting them for no apparent reason—so they need to be able to count on Mom to be in their corner, the person who loves them more than anyone else. Mom doesn't have to fix whatever it is; she just has to listen (and then pray).

That is a heavy load to carry. Thank God we don't have to carry it by ourselves. His plan all along was to walk this journey alongside us.

At some point, no matter how encouraging and affirming you've been to your kids, when they become teens they will try their wings and test the boundaries. At this point, their choices and mistakes will challenge you to keep alive the big picture—the vision—for their lives. If it hasn't happened yet, it will, even if those mistakes and failures aren't major crises. So how will you respond?

How will you remain confident when your child makes a mistake in life that brings consequences—even serious ones?

What if your daughter comes home pregnant or your son gets arrested for a DUI?

Will you pronounce their lives over or will you keep the flame of love and hope going?

Hopefully, you won't have to face issues as severe as these, but herein lies the truth: *Mothers are responsible to hold out hope for their children when everyone else has lost it.* How she responds to these moments speaks volumes about the level of a mother's faith and her own sense of value.

Over my two-plus decades of being a psychotherapist, I've had the opportunity to work with numerous families, especially religious ones. Many mothers whose husbands were in ministry or leadership in the church have shown up on my doorstep with a pregnant daughter.

What happens next is always telling.

More times than not, the mother informs me that she doesn't believe in abortion but that her situation is different. In my presence, she even tells the daughter that if the girl has the baby,

her life will be over,
        her dreams gone.

In most circumstances the mother goes on to say that if the daughter gives birth to this baby, she'll be on her own. Having spoken with numerous Crisis Pregnancy Center directors, I've discovered this is a common story among their clientele.

Now here is the question:

Who lost hope?

The teen was in crisis and shock and looked to her mother to be the face of hope in her most vulnerable time of life. Instead, she received rejection, control, and despair. This very issue is one reason why so many pregnant teens quit talking to their mothers and have abortions privately. They realize their mother's vision for them is based on an image or expectation—based on what they do, and not who they really are.

MISTAKES VS. FAILURE

When our children make mistakes, and they will, we have an opportunity to help them become wiser. A mistake isn't failure as long as teens learn something about themselves in the midst of their fall. The issue isn't what they did but who they can become as a result of this experience. Will they learn and grow into a healthy adult from the consequences of bad decisions in their teen years?

Mistakes can either define them or show them how God defines them.

Remember, our children must be defined by God's definition of them and love for them, not by their behavior or our fears. It is simply unfair to allow a season of development—adolescence—to frame their entire value, especially at a time when they are so desperately trying to figure out who they are and where they are headed.

Defining Value and Creating Confidence

This leads us to a deeper question: How do you define your value? Is it based upon *who you are* or *what you do*? How you define this for yourself will impact the value you place on your children and how they see their own value in your eyes and in God's.

We live in an era where people seek truth in many ways. In such a culture of "anything goes," it is important that we know the truth about God's attitude toward us, His opinion of us, and His unconditional love for us so we can model this to our children. Then our teenagers, who are constantly searching for identity, can find it in God because they see Him in us.

We can't teach our children principles and values that we haven't learned ourselves. If a mother struggles with her value and thinks her greatest contribution to her children's lives is what she does for them, then she has a problem. Her value to her children is who she is, period. No one will ever have the significance in her children's lives that she does.

Do you recall attending a program at school or church when your children were on stage?

Remember how they scanned the audience, looking for your face?

When they saw you, their face filled with relief, and maybe a big grin. At that moment, you were simply *being Mom*. You couldn't really do anything for them, but your presence was the confidence they needed not to run off stage. Your *presence* became their *confidence*.

This example allows us to ask several key questions:

- When you were a little girl, to whom did you look for hope and confidence?

- What was it like for you to know someone believed in you no matter what?

- What was it like for you if you had no one to love you unconditionally?

The answers to these questions will give you insight into your fears and struggles with unconditional love and vision keeping. You can't sustain a big-picture attitude and hold forth the vision for your children without believing in your own value before God.

The good news is that if you struggle with your sense of value, this is an area where God can step into your motherhood. As you have heard me say already, motherhood is God's way of showing us how inadequate we are and how much we truly need Him. He loves for us to be put into a place where we know we're in over our heads so we will be more likely to include Him in the equation of our parenting.

God wants to be present in our motherhood. After all, He created our children and placed them in our care. When God's presence becomes our confidence, our presence can be our children's confidence.

One of the observations I've made during years of providing therapy is that many mothers come from a wounded past. If a woman was raised by an intentional mother, she is indeed blessed and has her mother as a model by which to raise her own children. But if her mother was inadequate, she must overcome that experience in order to become an intentional mother to her own children. Otherwise she will be bogged down in the "moments" and unable to keep the vision for her kids.

However, when a "wounded" mother chooses to mother differently than she was parented, she breaks the pattern of dysfunction and opens a path for God to bring healing. I believe such healing is a gift of God specifically given because she intentionally chose to mother from a place that was new and challenging for her.

Once a mother begins to truly catch a glimpse of God's adoring love for her, that truth changes her.

It gives her a sense of value that her children catch from her.

It instills the confidence to hold on to the vision for her children because her faith is in the One who gave her those particular children.

When a mother begins to see that her faith is in Christ, and not her children or herself, the tension eases. This allows both mother and child to feel valued, and to focus on their own journey. Instilling this sense of value in your children frees them to learn the life lessons God needs them to grasp before they move to the next stage in life.

WISDOM IN SLOW MOTION

One way your child moves forward in adolescence is by testing his or her wings. Teenagers are forming their perceptions about life, which then provide the foundation for making decisions— both big and small. When a mother keeps the future vision for her child in the forefront, she can successfully reframe her own perception of her teenager's choices.

Instead of losing patience with our teenager's questionable decisions, we must remember that our child's life and maturity are still unfolding. Our kids need time and space to grow in the manner their heart and mind requires.

We need to support our teens, even though we may not agree with all their choices. Adolescence is the season in a person's life where one is truly learning to be responsible for decisions that may have consequences Mom can't fix. Our children can't become good decision makers without the opportunity to practice this in a safe environment.

When Neil and I attended orientation for our daughter's college, the dean of students made an interesting observation. She suggested that we encourage our incoming freshman to take one or two morning classes. She went on to say that most students have been programmed—from elementary school through high-school—with so many activities and busy schedules that when they get to college they struggle with scheduling time on their own. They've just left high-school, a highly structured experience with athletics, academics, community service, part-time jobs, and so on. Now in college, students have so much time on their hands, they don't know what to do with themselves.

The dean told us that because incoming freshmen are used to their lives being dictated to them, they haven't learned to think things through personally. As a result, they've been on automatic pilot for so long they crash and burn when they arrive at college.

It is extremely important for us to seize this time in their life— adolescence—to help them process the real issues of life. In this way, they learn to look at the big picture for their lives as well.

Decision making is an integral part of maturing into an adult. If our children can't make their mistakes while under our roof, we truly do them a disservice. Choices have consequences and benefits. Children need to learn this truth while they're evolving. They need to learn these lessons in an environment that allows them to maximize the moment instead of focusing on being afraid of how we will respond to their bad decisions.

If we make their mistakes about us instead of them, we delay the life lesson and give them the message that we aren't wise enough to handle the issues they face (or maybe create). When we keep the focus of our teens' choices on their lives, not ours, they see our true motives—our heart and vision for their lives—and as a result, they're more likely to trust us.

Teenagers will test their mothers with the decisions they make.

My son was my tester. You may have one of these too—if not now, later.

I reminded Taylor of his curfew whenever he left the house, and he was fine with it until he reached the end of the driveway. About an hour before curfew, he'd call and ask for an extension.

As I held my ground on my end of the phone, he'd argue with me in front of his friends about how unfair I was. I always reiterated my position and usually told him that if he needed more time, he should have started earlier in the day. I often ended these conversations with something like, "The curfew stands as is!"

Of course I waited up for his arrival home because I needed to make sure that (1) he got home safely and (2) he obeyed me. Without exception, Taylor always walked in the door at the time of curfew with a "Hey, Mom. How are you doing?" He was always just fine—no attitude. But he had to call me in front of his friends, lose the battle, and then come home.

My son needed me to stand my ground without busting his chops. He needed to make me the bad guy in front of his friends, and I was more than willing to be that for him.

(Here is a tip for you. When your teens get older, set the alarm for the agreed-upon curfew. They have to get in and turn off the clock before it goes off. If they don't succeed, they have to pay you a dollar for every minute they're late or lose a night out per minute. Curfew will be a nonissue with this tactic.)

I had to stand firm with Taylor so he could learn how to make the right decisions. If I'd given in, he would not have known where the boundaries were. Adolescents need boundaries in order to discover how to make their way as adults in this world. If they don't learn how to make wise decisions in a place where we can offer support and be a buffer, they will have much more difficulty doing so out in the world with little protection.

Being a wall for our teens to bounce against is significant for them. It provides a foundation that doesn't move when everything else in their life is constantly shifting. If we stand strong and firm while being kind and supportive, it will give them strength, security, and hope as they discover who they are and how to make decisions in life.

My image of adolescents is that they are like jiggly gelatin. The firming process lasts well into the midtwenties for girls and near thirty for guys. As you can see, adolescence just gets the process jump-started. But it is crucial because it will impact the severity of the bumps and bruises during their time of identity formation.

Adolescence doesn't have to be the scary picture we dread when our kids are young. It is a crucial time in their lives and can be a wonderful time in ours when we appreciate, respect, and understand where they are in this experience called life.

How do we as mothers keep the vision for our children in mind? If you're having trouble doing so with your teens, perhaps you need to reflect on your own childhood, to see what history you bring to your relationship with your teen. Your connection to your mother impacts you in one way or the other—to be a better mother than she was, or as good.

Looking at your own journey gives you a new appreciation for where your teens are now. It will also help you to keep the big picture of their journey—the vision—at the forefront of your mind. Being intentional always pays off. It just may be awhile before you receive the reward. However, peace can be yours when you walk through the deep waters, because you will know that this is a journey for your children, not their definition.

As vision keepers for our children, we must remember that God is a vision keeper for us. He never gives up on us and always sees our future—and that of our children—through the filter of a merciful and loving heart.

Faith Points

*. . . being confident of this, that he who began a good work
in you will carry it on to completion until the day of Christ Jesus.*

~ Philippians 1:6 ~

Isn't it good that God doesn't stop believing in us when we're the most vulnerable? Likewise, parents are called to keep the hope, faith, and vision alive for their teens when they're struggling. Take a moment and ask God to help you see them from His perspective. It will give you more compassion, greater insight, and a gentler spirit.

1. What issue with your child is keeping your eyes off the vision for his or her life?

2. What vision do you have for each of your children?

3. What practical thing can you do to remind yourself of the vision for your child when you're tempted to get bogged down in fear or anxiety about the "here and now"?

4. What recent mistake has your child made, and how can you help him or her learn from it?

5. What was the greatest insight you gained from this chapter, and how can you put it to use today?

4

BECOME A THINKING MOM
Principle 4: Be Intentional about Developing Emotional Intelligence

In 1981 several university professors conducted a study of valedictorians and salutatorians in the state of Illinois, following them through college into their initial careers. Surprisingly, though these students performed well in college, by the time they reached their midtwenties, they were merely average in their level of professional success.[1]

In Daniel Goleman's book *Emotional Intelligence*, he quotes Karen Arnold, one of the professors who tracked these academic performers: "To know that a student is a valedictorian is to know only that he or she is exceedingly good at achievement as measured by grades. It tells you nothing about how they react to the vicissitudes of life."[2]

In other words, these valedictorians and salutatorians knew how to be good students.

That's it.

Not great people,
 with great character,
  with great heart and soul.

Just good students.

Why, then, do we spend so much time investing in our children's academic success yet come up short in developing the other parts of their lives—the parts with a greater long-term impact on their quality of life and relationships?

Because we don't know we are missing the boat.

And in some ways, focusing on academics is easier.

We think we're directing our efforts in the right places, but the truth is, we don't invest in the areas of the greatest impact on our children's *quality* of life. While nothing is wrong with a mother ensuring her child's potential, she will carry many regrets if she places the lion's share of her energy into an area that will not produce long-term results.

Mothers also tackle academic challenges more easily because they feel a greater sense of mastery over this part of their kids' lives. Academics are measurable; moms can see immediate results and know where to go for assistance. Tutors, learning centers, and specialty groups are readily available resources for us to tap into when our children battle a learning issue.

But where do we go when emotional issues surface in our kids?

Most mothers go into denial.

Then we escape into fear.

Mothers begin to feel inadequate, overwhelmed, and frustrated when they have to deal with their children's emotional issues. These feelings surface in us because: (1) we don't understand why the emotions have arisen, and (2) these issues cause us to wonder whether we are good mothers. We also struggle because our children's feelings may not fit into our "logic box." They simply don't make sense to us.

But that's not the point.

Our children's feelings don't need to make sense to us.

Our job is to recognize our children's emotions—and then to hear them, accept them, and help our kids process them. It isn't our job to fix their feelings, justify their feelings, or deem them worthy.

Let's step back and explore this crucial step in motherhood so we don't lose the opportunity and privilege to create a foundation to help them become healthy adults. We need to do more than embrace what will help them with their careers. We must spend our time and energy in the areas that will help them with their *lives*.

CHRIST'S EXAMPLE

All of life is about relationships.

Jesus modeled that belief by how He prioritized relationships in the three short years He had to make a difference while on earth. Unlike His religious counterparts, Christ focused on the heart of faith and what it meant to the lives He encountered. He genuinely cared about every person with whom He experienced human life.

Jesus didn't pursue the most academically successful men as His disciples. In fact, the twelve He selected didn't cut it in the rabbinical system of their day. They were the underachievers of their time when it came to religious education.

Instead, Jesus Christ sought out those who were diverse in their levels of relationships and experiences. These twelve men would be credited with changing the world for Christ; they traveled all across the lands, teaching, preaching, and ministering to people they didn't know.

They had to possess great people skills to impact so many people in such a short amount of time. Yet their knowledge of Christ grew out of their *relationship* with Him, not a book or school.

Jesus knew what He was doing as He trained the disciples. Time and time again He modeled the things that really mattered:

loving people unconditionally,
> accepting people in spite of what others thought, and
> > meeting people in their place of need.

Jesus really understood the power of relationships, and until His last moment on earth, He modeled for us a perfect portrait of intimate, emotionally healthy relationships.

Jesus wants us to invest in the things that really matter. Rules, earthly success, possessions, and so on, have meaning but aren't life changing. Jesus knows that it doesn't matter if people obtain knowledge if they don't first possess heart, character, and faith.

Now let's switch gears to children.

Kids are relational. They're born that way. Yet in order for them to achieve their optimal level of human interaction and blessing, we must make the relationship area of their life a main priority. We call this area *emotional intelligence.*

DEFINING EMOTIONAL INTELLIGENCE

Before I can proceed with your options in teaching your child about emotional intelligence, I owe you an explanation of emotional intelligence (EQ). I am sure you won't be surprised by any particular characteristic, but you may not have put them together collectively. Emotional intelligence includes:

1. *Knowing one's emotions*: Recognizing a feeling as it happens. The ability to identify feelings from moment to moment is critical for possessing insight into others as well as one's self. "People with greater certainty about their feelings are better pilots of their lives."[3]

2. *Managing emotions*: This skill indicates how well children can comfort themselves in the midst of stress, adversity, despair, and other difficult feelings. A child who fails at this skill has difficulty bouncing back from emotional

issues, while those who learn how to self-sooth recover quickly.

3. *Motivating oneself*: Delaying instant gratification and controlling impulses are strong indicators that a child will be able to focus on a long-term goal. Children with this skill possess a higher probability of succeeding in whatever they undertake.

4. *Recognizing emotions in others*: Empathy is a necessary skill for children to enjoy effective relationships. Children who possess this ability pick up on the subtle social cues other kids use to communicate with one another.

5. *Handling relationships*: This skill allows a child to manage the playground, classroom, or athletic field with his or her personal skills instead of academic or athletic abilities. These skills impact popularity as well as leadership and interpersonal competency.[4]

These five characteristics form the core indicators to predict your child's future judgments and relationship healthiness. Your child's ability to master these emotional skills will positively impact your child's ability to select good friends, recognize risky decisions, and optimize his or her relationships.

Now, let's be honest.

Moms worry about their kids when they don't get along with other children their age.

> We also grow concerned when they struggle with insensitivity, aloofness, and/or overreaction.

>> Mostly, we fail to recognize how hard it is for our children to identify their feelings.

Many children I've known have trouble articulating their emotions. When asked how they feel, their typical response is, "I don't know." One reason for their reaction might be that few parents ever ask their children how they feel. You would be surprised at how rare that question is posed to a child.

By the way, when is the last time you asked your child that question?

We can begin asking our kids about their feelings the minute they begin to talk. They may not have the vocabulary to respond, but we need practice asking. They will eventually learn how to answer. We want them to understand that feelings aren't right or wrong, good or bad. It's our job simply to help them identify their feelings.

What's another reason we fail to ask this crucial question? We haven't appreciated its relevance to our children's long-term happiness, rather than only their immediate internal peacefulness. Because they're young, we tend to overlook their feelings. We assume their emotions will change quickly. Most of the time, we think if we ignore them for a few minutes, their uncomfortable feelings will go away.

They don't go away.

They go underground.

Later they might surface in a temper tantrum, an overreaction, or sullenness. But our kids' feelings don't go away.

Moms, wake up to the incredible opportunity we have to develop our children emotionally. If we don't take the time to cultivate this dimension of our children's hearts, we will experience greater challenges when they are teens.

I've often sat in my office across from a teenager when the only response I receive is, "I don't know." I often ask their mothers if this is an unusual response or a typical one. Without exception, they tell me it is their child's typical answer when asked how they feel.

Why?

Why do we allow our teens to not know how they feel? Why is it okay to give them a pass on that question when we won't take that same response when we ask them why they didn't turn in their homework?

For one thing, we don't think.

We don't push beyond the immediate moment to look into the big-picture future to see where our current experience might take us. Either we're too busy, or we're in the midst of a thousand things so we don't have time, or it doesn't seem to be that big of a deal.

In many cases, it isn't a "big deal." However, we easily establish patterns of response because we're not paying attention and thinking about each situation's significance in our child's life—now and later.

Many times in therapy I've worked with parents who told me that, looking back, they saw the signs and symptoms of issues that were brewing with their children, but they failed to connect the dots. When pushed as to how or why they missed the signs in their kids, their response is, "I didn't think it through."

"I didn't think it through."

Have you ever said that?

Most of us have. But we need to wake up and realize that answer will come back to hurt us—and our kids—if we use it too frequently. The truth is, if we don't "think through" our parenting, we likely won't teach our children to become thinking people.

Herein lies one of our great issues. Some of us moms are scared to push through the uncomfortable places. Our fear causes our thinking to shut down. As a result, we don't push our kids to think through issues either.

LET'S THINK IT THROUGH

Thinking is an assumption as well as a fact. It's something our brain must do in order for us to function. However, the quality of our functioning depends on how well we think and if we cultivate the *habit* of thinking well.

But let's face it, some people think only enough to get by. We assume they're thinking because they walk around, they breathe, they speak. But true thinking isn't just bare-minimum, brain-keeping-us-alive thoughts. Just because someone—you or your child—is standing upright and functioning doesn't mean he or she is thinking through the small and big decisions of life. Some people let life just come along and roll past them without ever considering how circumstances, decisions, or a lack of decision making affects them and those around them.

We need to engage with life.

Do you want your child to be a nonthinker? Of course not.

But your child won't learn to think if you don't think. Thinking not only helps us and our children learn to make decisions; it helps us develop emotional intelligence.

Thinking is a decision we make to examine all outcomes, processes, and possibilities in a given situation.

For the purpose of this principle, let me explain how an intentional mother will define and exercise thinking with her children and teens.

An intentional mother seizes the opportunity to use life moments to teach her child or teen a lesson, skill, or insight that is bigger than the actual moment. She recognizes that immediate answers aren't always the best solution, and that her best mothering may take place over time. An intentional mother embraces time as an ally, not an enemy.

Let me illustrate.

When Taylor was twelve, he went on a church camping trip with a group of boys he had known all his life. One of these boys had always annoyed my son. Taylor and I often discussed different tactics he could use to deal with this child. To this point, we had not faced any major issues in their relationship.

While on this trip, this boy, Charlie, continued his antics toward Taylor. As a result of his frustration, Taylor finally called him a name. Fortunately, it wasn't a "bad" name, but it wasn't nice either.

When I arrived to pick up Taylor from the camping trip, Charlie's father approached me about the incident. "I think you should make Taylor apologize to my son," this indignant dad remarked. I assured him I would talk to Taylor and deal with him accordingly.

On the drive home I asked Taylor about the incident. He admitted to calling Charlie an unkind name, but he wasn't ready to apologize. I prayed with Taylor when we got home. I didn't use this prayer to beat him up or to make him change. I thanked God for letting Taylor be my son and I asked God to speak to his heart. I also thanked God for how He would use this experience in Taylor's life to show him how much God loved him.

The next day, Charlie's father approached me again to ask me if I was going to make Taylor apologize.

I told him no.

The father was flabbergasted.

I explained my position. "My job as a mother is to teach Taylor what is right and wrong, show him God's heart, and trust that the Holy Spirit will convict him when he has sinned. I can bring Taylor over here right now and make him apologize to your son, but it won't be sincere. He will do it out of obedience to me, not because he has a right heart. I am more interested in raising a right-hearted man than another religious Pharisee."

This father wasn't happy with me.

But it didn't matter. There was a bigger picture in this situation, and I didn't want to miss the chance to see God work in my son's life.

I continued to pray for Taylor about this issue, but I didn't bring it up again with my son. Every once and awhile this father made another comment. I simply ignored him.

Almost six months after the camping incident, Taylor got into the car one Sunday morning and said, "Mom, I apologized to Charlie for calling him that name. I was wrong and I shouldn't have done that."

My heart melted.

"Taylor, I am always proud of you, but today I am proud *for* you. Nothing feels better than righting a wrong with a friend," I told him.

Six months.

Let me say this again.

Six months.

That is a long time in a child's life for a lesson to unfold. But it takes time for some children and teens to process through an experience. Every child is different, so an experience like this one might not work for your kids. Whatever your situation, the point is that our best mothering includes those moments when we recognize the importance of living through and learning from our kids' life experiences rather than simply enduring them.

Children and adolescents need time to think through their options, choices, consequences, benefits, and outcomes. Thinking is a *skill* that requires time, patience, and opportunity. Practice doesn't necessarily make perfect, but it does improve their odds at making better decisions.

Children and teens who become good thinkers are also more likely to have the courage to say no to poor choices and temptation. They learn to tap into logic instead of emotion when you've taught them to think instead of react.

Intentional mothers are thinking mothers; we must think our way through the motherhood journey, and that may be the most challenging part of our journey. We have to be willing to go to the deeper layers of our own thoughts and feelings to effectively lead our children to the same place.

IDENTIFY EMOTIONS

In the beginning of this chapter, I outlined the ingredients of emotional intelligence. The first step is *awareness of feelings*. Here is where I find many mothers identify their first obstacle in their own struggle with emotional intelligence.

If a mother can't identify her own emotions, or sends them underground, she will have difficulty being sensitive to her children's feelings. This disconnection communicates a message to her children that Mom isn't emotionally present or available.

I recommend that every mother see the movie classic *Ordinary People*. This Oscar-winning film is a perfect example of a mother whose emotional walls are up so high that she can't see anyone's pain except her own, including her son's. The movie takes viewers through a journey of what happens to this woman's teenage son as a result of her unwillingness to access her own heart so she can touch his. While this film is painful to watch, it is an amazing reminder about what can happen to our kids when we're unwilling to work on our own emotional health.

An intentional mother recognizes that her children may be the vehicle God uses to bring healing into her life. Because she wants her children to be emotionally healthy and spiritually whole, she willingly faces the challenge of her own emotional baggage so that she doesn't pass it to the next generation. She recognizes that her *example* is more important than her *words,* and that her *interactions* with her children provide greater potential impact on their future relationships than her *instruction.*

One consideration every mother needs to remember is that each child is different, and some children require more work than others. Even in healthy circumstances, you may find yourself with an introverted child who struggles to talk about his emotions. Don't let that deter you. Just because he feels uncomfortable doesn't mean he can't learn a feeling vocabulary.

One observation I've made over my years of working with families is the type of vocabulary used in their personal interactions. I can spend only five minutes with a family and tell you whether they are comfortable sharing their emotions.

How is that possible?

Listen to the conversation in your home one morning at breakfast, in the car, or before bedtime. As you listen, notice how often your family uses words that denote emotion. For example, when your children bicker, do they say, "Stop doing that, it makes me mad," or do they just complain about their sibling. If your child cries and you ask her why, or what's wrong, does she answer with feeling words such as "I'm sad," "My feelings are hurt," or "I'm frustrated," or does she only tell you the "facts" of her problem?

What language does your family use? Factual words or feeling words?

In many families, you could record conversations all day long and never once hear a word that describes a feeling or emotion.

Yet that doesn't mean the family isn't experiencing emotion.

It simply means their feelings aren't identified or acknowledged.

Intentional mothers use "feeling words" in their daily exchanges with family members. They don't hesitate to say, "How did you feel when you stole that cookie?" or "What do you feel like when you're misunderstood?" These types of questions invite our children to tap into their feelings and learn how to express emotions with their words, not just their behavior.

A child or teen with a good command of an emotionally laden vocabulary is more expressive in relationships as well as academics. This expressiveness will show up in their conversations, writings, and subjects that require creativity. This is only one example of how children benefit when a mother creates an atmosphere of emotional healthiness.

Now, would it have dawned on you that emotional sensitivity and health can impact your child academically? If you were like most moms, you would have connected those dots if you thought about it.

Notice what I just wrote.

If you *thought* about it.

BE PRESENT

Therein lies the issue. Most of the time we don't stay with a thought long enough to let it connect to anything. We're so rushed and active with well-meaning activities that we miss the deeper life issues that can have a huge impact on the quality of our lives and our children's health. We've stopped being *present* with our children, even in their presence.

A new concept is floating around our culture. This new phenomenon contributes to increasingly empty parent-child interaction. It is called *present absence*.

Let me explain.

A mother is attending her child's Little League game or dance lesson. While on the field or in the studio, she spends her time on her cell phone chatting with her friends, making plans, dealing with issues, or some other life matter. Whenever her child looks over toward his or her mother to gain a sense of support and encouragement, instead that child sees that Mom's attention is directed toward a phone conversation. She isn't engaged with her child even though she's present.

Thus, while the mother can satisfy her feelings of "being there" for her child, she isn't really "there" for her child.

She is *present absent*—her body is present but her attention and energy are other-directed and not child-focused.

I am not saying that we have to "fast" from the phone (which I've done, by the way) during every practice, game, or rehearsal, but I do think we need to awaken to the amount of time we spend with our children when we're not actually "with" our children.

Intentional mothers recognize that thinking is a value that requires time, attention, and priority.

You must learn to be actively present with your children. Mothers who learn to be available for their children have more time to think through the emotional issues that arise every day. Intentional mothers who learn to think, and therefore value their own emotional health, increase their children's potential for a higher level of emotional intelligence.

PAY ATTENTION

Peter, one of Jesus' disciples, studied under Christ for three years before being left to go it on his own. During that time, Jesus consistently dealt with Peter's impetuous personality. Peter reacted, lied, denied, and whined during the time he was mentored. Jesus always reeled him back in with truth, love, and patience.

Fortunately for all of us, we see the outcome of the time Christ spent with Peter and the impact Jesus had on teaching Peter to trust Him with his whole heart and soul. About this impetuous man Jesus said, "On this rock, I will build my church."[5]

That should give all of us hope.

Especially if we are raising children who have difficulty managing their emotions and behavior in a healthy manner.

Most of us mothers will need to pay attention to our children's ability to cope and manage life. Some of our kids handle emotions quite well, while others are drama queens (or kings) who make everything a crisis. When you have a child like this, consider it an opportunity to pay attention to what's happening when she exhibits this behavior. It's another chance to learn about your child.

Dramatic behaviors often get on a mom's nerves because such actions seem manipulative, whiney, and controlling. While dramatic behaviors may contain elements of such negative motivations, I'm more interested in your looking for *patterns* that may arise in your child's reactions. If your child repeats these actions, he or she is holding out a clue, a cry for help in this area, not just tolerance.

Everyone has a bad day, overreacts, and melts down now and again. But if one of your children begins to show a pattern of such behavior—being hysterical, on edge, and/or unable to manage even the simplest of tasks—there's a reason for their extreme reactions. Emotions are dominating the child's behavior, thoughts, and feelings. Logic is out the window. The child is unable to rationally respond to situations. You need to understand the reason behind their irrational behavior.

There's always a reason why children do what they do. However, don't expect your children to always know what that reason is.

That's why they have you.

One of your jobs is to help them figure out the issues.

On many occasions, I've watched parents become annoyed because of a problem their kids could not articulate. Instead of reacting in anger or frustration, parents must recognize that talking, time, and understanding will lead them down the path to the correct revelation. Once the problem is revealed, solutions can be found.

ADDITIONAL EQ QUALITIES

Two more dynamics in raising emotionally healthy children are *delayed gratification* and *internal motivation*. These two qualities are easier to implement in children than one would imagine, but they do require determination and time.

We live in a world of instant gratification—microwave meals, drive-thrus, ATMs, Internet. Our kids are growing up in a culture where almost any desire that pops into their head can be fulfilled instantaneously.

Years ago, American culture had no instant gratification. When a kid grew up on a farm, he understood the natural order of things, the rhythm of life, the principle of sowing and reaping. Crops were planted in the spring and harvested in the fall. Children learned how to wait.

We don't teach that today. And when they don't know how to wait for something, they don't understand the value of investing in a goal, a desire, a relationship.

Take the transition from high-school to college, for example. High-school seniors cannot simply get into their college of choice if they've not been preparing for the application process for years—through GPAs, community service, standardized testing, and extracurricular activities. Your teen must start thinking in middle school about how to invest his or her time and abilities into the long-term college goal.

Athletes have known this for years. They spend hours in training every day, sacrificing other things in life, in order to pursue a dream. There is no instant gratification, only the personal satisfaction of thinking about how to invest in an achievement that will bring fruit down the road.

So how do we teach delayed gratification? When your children are young, don't always give them everything they ask for. Encourage them to save their allowance to buy something they want—to work for things they desire instead of receiving something for nothing.

Families who say a dinnertime blessing before anyone can eat teach their kids delayed gratification. Having a child wait to leave the table until everyone is finished is not only good manners but also teaches a child to wait patiently.

There are many other ways to practice delayed gratification, but all of them require intentionality. Teaching your children this value also teaches them how to wait on God when they've prayed for something. God doesn't always answer our prayers immediately. He will answer them when His time is perfect and complete.

Internal motivation is another element that gives a child a higher probability of emotional healthiness. Motivation can be tricky, because every child has a different set of stimuli that drives him or her. But as I mentioned in principle 2, when a mother is a student of her child, she learns to discern what that drive may be.

Children and teens who are internally motivated are more likely to take responsibility for themselves, are more mature, and recognize the consequences and benefits of their choices.

When I homeschooled my children, I quickly realized that for this approach to work effectively, I needed to teach them they were responsible for their schoolwork. I did the lesson plans, taught them certain materials, and provided extracurricular activities to help their learning come alive. However, I made sure my kids took responsibility for completing their assignments.

As a result, when they returned to private school, both my children immediately assumed responsibility for homework, assignments, and projects. I was grateful I didn't have to push, threaten, and cajole them into completing their work.

They just did it.

Life won't always produce instantaneous results. We need to teach our children how to invest, how to wait for the most important things of life. Otherwise they won't make wise decisions about education, careers, mates—life. They must learn to choose what is right and true instead of what is easy and popular.

I hope by now you, too, see a pattern of the benefits of thinking through the issues that can so quickly get lost in the daily routine of life as a mom. Your children may fight you at times, but the blessings you'll all gain later will be worth it.

FROM THE PLAYGROUND TO THE CORPORATE WORLD

As an executive coach in the corporate world, I've experienced moments when I thought I was on the playground instead of inside the brain trust of a Fortune 500 company. I've watched in amazement as men and women who make incredible salaries, oversee thousands of employees, and have great influence in the corporate world relate to people on an immature and childish level.

I've also observed "minityrants," bosses who rule as if they're two years old. These people typically have high turnover among their staff, make extreme demands, and take no responsibility for their behavior. They always claim to be victims and rule with a command-and-control mentality.

In whatever form they come, such emotionally immature people live fretfully and create stress for all those around them daily. Yet in most cases, they're totally unaware of their impact on others. The same dynamics that played out in high-school—or worse yet, on the elementary-school playground—show up in the corporate world, because some people never grew up emotionally.

While their bodies might age, their emotions are stuck, and they hurt many people with:

> their juvenile antics,
>> bully tactics, and
>>> jocklike mentality.

Is this the type of adult you want your child to become? Of course not.

One of the reasons such people hurt others is that they don't recognize the power of their position, nor do they understand the damage their immaturity causes their subordinates. Many of them don't know how to read the emotions of others, and many subordinates work hard to hide from their bosses to prevent being wounded or emotionally injured.

People who experience the greatest joy in their relationships are those who feel safe, feel valued, and have purpose. On the other hand, when a person cannot give respect to others, it shows up somewhere in their relationships, and it probably won't be pretty.

I don't want you to feel too much pressure, but here is the truth:

Emotional maturity begins in childhood with how parents relate, speak, listen, touch, and pay attention to their children. If we're sensitive to our kids' emotional needs, they will develop awareness and sensitivity to others, because that will be their definition of *normal*.

When we fail to teach our children their impact on others, it can follow them throughout life. In many cases, they won't outgrow emotional immaturity.

Some groups of children—for instance, those who've been diagnosed with certain neurological or developmental conditions—struggle with the ability to read other people's emotions and feelings. The nature of their neurological problem is that they're not wired with the ability to empathize or read social cues. They can be insensitive, disconnected, and emotionally cold.

However, they have a reason for being the way they are. It is not due to emotional ineptness from the child's family interactions. It is simply the way they were born.

These children, as well as children with other disabilities, especially need their mothers to be emotionally healthy so they have a good chance of learning how to assimilate well into the world. Their lack of emotional availability is extremely demanding. An unhealthy mother will lose hope, feel perpetually frustrated, and fail to see a Kingdom vision for that child.

Raising a child with special needs is draining, so if you fall into this category, don't hesitate to identify and utilize available emotional, educational, and spiritual support for yourself and your child.

Out of their own emotional health, intentional mothers can teach their children how to see others with "thinking" eyes. Whether a child has emotional deficits or just needs a good example, your responsibility is to help them become true, mature, emotionally healthy adults. They will be blessed with lasting, deep relationships.

THE END RESULT

Intentional mothers recognize that motherhood requires them to be present and accounted for throughout the journey. When mothers check their brains into the process and refuse to have a survivor mentality, the benefits far outweigh the difficulties.

Our children will be blessed when we help them develop emotional intelligence. This gives them a huge lead into well-adjusted living, good decision making, and internal confidence.

When a mother is insensitive, she creates issues for God. Her children won't learn to be sensitive to His voice.

But when a mother makes it her priority to develop her children emotionally, she raises people who will think, have awareness of themselves and others, and have access to their own hearts, which makes God's job easier. He won't have to penetrate a wall to be heard within their hearts.

Should you decide to raise a thinking child, please be aware that he or she may grow up to think differently from you. Don't let that scare you; the advantages far outweigh the disadvantages. Thinking children are emotionally intelligent children, and they'll make you a better person, be more likely to make good decisions, and exude greater confidence as an adult.

Most importantly, when you invest in thinking about and teaching your children emotional intelligence, you will enjoy your motherhood journey with greater contentment and appreciation. Life's moments have more meaning, and you experience greater depth in your relationships that will bless you and give you incredible peace.

When you raise emotionally healthy children, you're well on the road of raising your children with no regrets.

FAITH POINTS

*If you call out for insight
and cry aloud for understanding,
and if you look for it as for silver
and search for it as for hidden treasure,
then you will understand the fear of the* LORD
*and find the knowledge of God.
For the* LORD *gives wisdom,
and from his mouth come knowledge
and understanding.*

~ Proverbs 2:3–6 ~

This chapter challenges us to think before we speak and to look at the layers of our children's heart and soul. When we are intentional in developing our children emotionally, it will enhance them spiritually and they will know God more deeply. They will see Him as a tender, gentle, feeling God, which makes Him a safe God.

1. How do you think your family's level of emotional expression affects your children, both positively and negatively?

2. How might you improve your own emotional intelligence?

3. When was the last time you didn't "think through" a situation involving one of your children? What was the result? How could you have a different result next time?

4. How can teaching delayed gratification help your children learn how to be more internally motivated in life?

5. In what ways can you become more present in your children's lives daily? Remember, each child is different, so how you choose to be more "present" with them will look different to each one.

6. What was the greatest insight you gained from this chapter, and how can you put it to use today?

5

RESPECT IS NECESSARY; HAPPINESS IS NOT

Principle 5: Be Intentional about Maintaining Your Position

In the twenty-five years I've been a psychotherapist, I've observed a shift in the way mothers address their children. One of the most frequent experiences I see, both inside and outside of my office, is very disturbing—and also a good predictor of future difficulties in a family (or with a child).

A typical scenario begins with a mother wanting her child to do something simple: sit on the couch, stop running inside the office, pick up a dropped object, and so on. The mother says something like, "Please sit down on the couch next to me." She initially tells the child to engage in the requested behavior in a kind, gentle voice.

The child ignores the mother, which is the equivalent of the child saying no.

The mother makes the request again, all to no avail.

The mother continues this exchange until something significant changes. That change can be as simple as Mom's voice tone or as obvious as a physical enforcement of the requested behavior. Usually by the time the child obeys, many things have transpired. Most of them aren't good.

In most such scenarios, the mother tries to make her child happy about obeying her.

107

Did you get that? Let me repeat it.

The mother tries to make her child happy about obeying her.

How realistic is that? By virtue of the definition of *obedience*, children have to willingly give up their opinion about what *they* want so they can do what their mom wants. And we expect them to be happy about that? I don't think so.

In these same scenarios, initially the mother's voice carries no sound of authority. She sounds tentative when she first makes her request, and her face reflects concern that she get the child through this experience with little damage.

The child quickly discovers that he is in charge, based on the confidence level of his mother's voice. As a result, the child then proceeds to push Mom to see how far he can go. By the time the mother is pushed over the edge, she resents her child, feels like a failure, and is emotionally drained. What makes this worse? Prospects for an improved future are bleak. If their interactions are this bad when the child is four or five, Mom might prefer to skip the next fifteen years!

All of this exhausting interaction is unnecessary in most parenting situations. Wouldn't you rather expend your energy enjoying your children instead of being worn out at the end of each day from constant pushing and pulling with them? Peaceful interaction with your kids is possible, but it requires you to step back and consider the underlying dynamics in your exchanges with your children.

Plain and simple, if your kids don't listen to you in their early years, forget having a relationship with them later. They will lose respect for you—and lack of respect is the kiss of death for relationships.

A mom with a four-year-old girl once came to see me for counsel. The mom asked her daughter to sit down next to her on the couch, but the girl completely ignored her. I could tell this little girl had been in charge way too long; this experience was going to be like breaking a stallion. So I told the mom we were going to start by immediately gaining control over her little girl. Mom needed to get ready for the ruckus.

Next, I told the child to sit down next to her mother and then I explained what would happen if she chose not to obey. She would have to go stand in the corner.

When the child did not listen, I promptly took her hand and led her to the corner. I explained to her mom that the girl would need to stay in the corner for four minutes without being out of control (a minute for every year of her age).

The child began to scream and yell.

Mom and I took turns standing with her in the corner.

This child pitched a fit for forty-five minutes.

Based upon the decibels of her screams, from outside our walls it probably sounded as if we were beating this child to death. The truth is, we were simply insisting that she obey us.

We didn't yell, scream, or holler.

We simply meant business.

We simply outlasted her.

And it blessed this little girl!

When she finally stood in the corner for four minutes without fighting us, I knelt down and told her I was proud of her for finally obeying us. I went on to tell her I knew that now she would obey the first time whenever her mom asked her to do something.

With that, the little girl came over to me, sniffling from her tears, put her arms around my neck, and collapsed into my arms.

She finally felt safe.

Someone was finally strong enough to stand up and be an adult so she could be a child.

I never had trouble with this girl obeying me again. Her mother also grew into the rightful position as a mother to her child on that day. While it would take some time for the mom to recognize and act like the parent her little girl needed, she eventually got it.

Mothers don't have to be mean or unkind to exercise their authority. They can even respectfully ask for the child to behave on the first exchange rather than making a demand. The issue is the mother's confidence in why she is doing what she is doing. Most important, it is crucial for mothers to examine the issue of the child's happiness in this experience.

Mothers often tell me they're concerned that their children won't like them if they make them behave. What is my response?

Oh well!

They'll get over it.

WHAT IS YOUR GOAL?

Everybody searches for happiness in one way or another. It is a desirable state and one we spend a tremendous amount of time, energy, and money trying to accomplish. Thus, the issue isn't whether we want happiness but how we define it. The other challenge for people in attaining happiness is that it looks different to each person. The problem is, we don't understand where happiness comes from.

Mothers have bought into a cultural phenomenon that makes parents responsible for their children's happiness. They feel burdened to provide their child every opportunity in every way so the child can become the best at whatever he or she desires. As a result, moms turn the world upside down to cater to their every whim so their kids will feel happy.

How do we moms do this?

We spend money we don't have,
        compromise sound judgment,
                and minimize our children's bad behavior for the sake of keeping peace.

All because we value making our children happy more than teaching them to obey.

If all this behavior isn't in the best interest of our children, why do moms do this? Whose need is really being met? Ours or our kids?

And where does respect come into play?

Does failure to make their children happy mean they aren't good mothers? Heaven forbid our children experience a little unhappiness in life.

Many moms are confused about their position. They believe mothers should be loving and kind, which will lead to their children being happy. But sometimes the position of motherhood requires tough decisions that are in our children's best interest. And I guarantee you these decisions won't always make them happy. When this happens to you, don't feel bad. You're not alone. Most mothers don't get any help in defining their priorities and understanding their position; they're simply told to do it all, have it all, and raise the complete child. So much emphasis is on raising *happy* children that moms are confused about this unrealistic emotional state.

You have heard me say this before, but it needs to be said again: A mother's priorities are to love her children well, discipline them fairly, teach them spiritual truth, believe in who God created them to be, provide opportunities for them to develop their unique wiring, and teach them their identity in Christ. While this sounds impossible, it takes place over a twenty-year-plus life cycle, one day at a time.

Notice that *happiness* isn't on the list.

I'm not saying you should be raising miserable children. However, we must distinguish between a *happy* life—which our culture leads people to believe is their entitlement—and a joyful or peaceful life—which isn't dependent on how much "stuff" we have or what we get to do. The right priority is to teach our children how to live in the moment they have and to be content with what they have.

We know that every mother wants her children to have happy lives. It bothers any right-minded mother if her child is unhappy and miserable most of the time. She has every right to be concerned and is wise to actively seek out the problems underlying her child's discontent.

The problem arises because our culture paints a picture of happy children, yet without providing clarity as to how that happiness occurs. Mothers feel an immense expectation to produce Einsteins, beauty queens, and Olympic athletes. The media tells us that great mothers stand in line at 3:00 A.M. to get their kid into the premier nursery school, or they sell their soul to pay for their children's private lessons in a specialized area of study.

As a result, mothers become confused about what makes a child happy. While they want happiness for their kids, they don't know how to create it.

The problem isn't how to make our kids happy. The problem is, mothers have made happiness the object of their focus. We are asking the wrong question. The question we should ask is, "What is my child's true need at this moment?"

If children aren't happy, perhaps they don't feel safe and secure. Or, they simply figured out that they are in charge, not Mom. So they scream for her to step in and take charge again so they can be the child.

It is not a mother's job to make her children happy.

> It is her job to love them well, discipline them fairly, and accept them unconditionally.

> It is her job to believe in a vision on their behalf, and to help them discover their passions, talents, and gifting to bring that God-given vision to life.

> *But it is not her job to make them happy.*

Believing so is an illusion, and that belief system will always prevent mothers from reaching an unrealistic goal.

Think about it a minute.

Are you always happy?

Do you know anyone who truly is constantly happy? These people don't exist, so why are you trying to create the unattainable for your children? If you embrace this thought pattern, you will create an emotionally unhealthy child, and set yourself up for a lifetime of guilt and frustration.

One of the great problems we have created in parenting is the thought that our children will be permanently damaged if they are unhappy or if life doesn't go their way. That is simply not true. If a child doesn't get his way, he isn't going to die, be permanently scarred, or have low self-worth.

He will, however, learn that life is about give-and-take, and that he isn't the center of the universe twenty-four hours a day, seven days a week. He will also learn that someone in his life loves him enough to teach him that saying no or requesting his obedience is another definition of love.

Happiness is a transitory state, changing like the wind. It is a feeling, one we all enjoy and embrace. Everyone likes the experience of being happy and it is a true blessing to see one's children experience it. Yet because happiness is momentary, we need to recognize that it is not sustainable in and of itself. It is not a reflection of self-worth, as are contentment, peacefulness, and hope. While important and desirous of being fulfilled, happiness is a fragment of life, but it is not to be our definition of living well.

So if happiness isn't what brings our children a sense of true well-being, what does?

Respect.

When mothers parent their children, they want to be intentional about doing so in a manner where respect and love are the foundation on which their relationship is built. If this happens in the relationship between a mother and child, the lifetime potential for them to navigate the later years with greater ease and trust increases dramatically. The sooner respect and love are established in the relationship, the easier it will be.

When mothers quit worrying about making their children happy and instead do what their children need, then kids discover contentment and safety. Setting limits and boundaries is healthy for children, and is a greater predictor of future happiness than pleasing them all the time. On top of all that, children are never satisfied when our goal is only to make them momentarily happy.

If you have ever taken your two- or three-year-old to the grocery store, you know what I mean. They're very touchy-feely at this age; they want things that look appealing. Typically, they start to reach for things as soon as their little arms will allow it. As you go down the aisles, they try to grab everything they see. You may relent, thinking that if you give them something, you'll satisfy them.

However, because their attention span is so short, they will be entertained only for a few minutes—until they pass by something more exciting. Then, they forget whatever is in their hands and begin reaching again. The game continues until one of two things happens: (1) you give them everything they reach for and walk out with things you—and they—don't need, or (2) you teach them the concept of "no."

Making a child happy does not mean he or she will cooperate with you, as the above-mentioned example points out. However, teaching them boundaries creates respect for authority and teaches them to value and appreciate what they do have. Through boundaries, children learn that happiness is not about what they possess, but is instead a contented state of mind that gives meaning and security to their lives.

Intentional mothers recognize that their goal for their children is long-term security and the development of a healthy, confident person. They understand that respect, when taught to their children all along the way, has long-term benefits for the child as well as their relationship with Mom.

LISTENING TO YOUR CHILDREN

In today's American culture, many children fall into two major categories: they're either taught they're the center of the universe or emotionally left to raise themselves. A smaller, less-practiced category arises from children with intentional mothers. Hope lies with these moms.

Mothers who recognize that respect begins in infancy will experience huge dividends with their children.

Such children know when a mother is listening to them and taking them seriously.

> They feel the honor when a mother takes the time to look them in the eye and acknowledge their questions.

> > Their self-worth increases when a mother believes what they say until proven otherwise.

Intentional mothers must grasp the concept that before respect can be received from their children, it first must be given to their children. If we give our children respect when they are little, they will give it to us when they are big.

Have you ever noticed how most adults believe another adult's word before they believe the word of a child?

Why is that?

What happens along the journey that causes us to distrust what our children tell us?

When my daughter was around eleven or twelve, a sweet, kind woman came into our family's life. Being in a ministry family affords you an opportunity to experience many people along life's journey—many of whom teach you valuable lessons. Our friend LeAnn became one of those lessons.

LeAnn was a teacher in one of the children's mission groups in our church. As a result, she had a lot of contact with Tiffany. She'd never been married, she loved children and animals, and she had a gentle, sweet demeanor. LeAnn also was a victim of severe abuse as a child, which had caused serious boundary confusion for her. I knew her history quite well, but I also knew she was working diligently to get a handle on her issues.

Our family befriended LeAnn, and she adored our children. Tiffany—being my compliant, easy child—was always responsive and polite toward her. However, as time went by, I sensed that Tiffany was becoming increasingly uncomfortable with LeAnn.

At first I encouraged Tiffany to politely let LeAnn know about her discomfort. I offered to be present when my daughter told our friend how she felt. I also went to LeAnn myself on several occasions to express my concerns about her emotional boundary violations and lack of respect for Tiffany's space. She was asking too much from Tiffany, and things finally came to a head.

My ever-patient daughter finally came to me in desperation and told me, "Mom, I love Miss LeAnn, but I can't deal with her right now. I know she means well but I just need her to stay out of my life because she can't seem to hear me when I tell her how I feel. I don't want to hurt her feelings, Mom, but I can't deal with her right now."

I knew that for Tiffany to ask something this drastic of me, it was extremely important that I respond to her request.

I knew this meant LeAnn would not be visiting our home for a while, and I knew it would upset LeAnn. I also knew this request was difficult for my daughter. She'd never asked me for anything like this, but I knew her well enough to know I needed to pay attention to her heart's need.

I told LeAnn that she could not be part of our inner circle for a season of time, and that I was setting this boundary out of respect for my daughter.

The break was uncomfortable for LeAnn, and she was sad to realize she'd neglected to hear Tiffany's needs and boundaries. All of us later looked back on this experience and realized we grew from it. The journey lasted almost two years, but during that time, God provided amazing healing in LeAnn's life.

For Tiffany and me, it was another opportunity for God to deepen our bond. She knew I had heard her and that I appropriately placed her needs before those of the adults in our lives. I am happy to say that the relationship between Tiffany and LeAnn now is endearing to both of them.

Too often, a child or teen's voice goes unheard because we somehow think it inappropriate to choose our child's thoughts and interpretations over those of an adult. Not that our children should always rule in decisions between another adult and them. However, experience, our history with others, and God will reveal how we should proceed in such times. Even if you believe an adult's interpretations of an event or experience, that doesn't mean your child or teen doesn't deserve to feel respected by being heard.

I recently counseled several boys who had gotten into trouble at school and received detentions. They were upset with the assistant principal—but for reasons one might not expect. The boys told me they never got the opportunity to explain why they had missed class. They were more than willing to serve detention, but their anger and frustration resulted from not having a chance to be heard. It all came down to a lack of respect.

Sometimes parents must fight for their children's honor and respect. When kids know you take them seriously, it deepens their confidence in themselves. That, dear mother, is the making of a healthy person.

Respect creates trust and trust yields respect.

Intentional mothers recognize that the early years of a child's life impact their relationship with the child later on. An intentional mother understands that maintaining respect as a priority will serve her well when her child's issues become more complex and challenging.

If you respect your children when they are young, your teens will respect you when they are older. That respect equates to openness, honesty, and vulnerability.

Submission can be commanded.

Obedience can be demanded.

Respect must be earned.

EARNING RESPECT

One way moms earn respect is by being willing to listen to their children—no matter the conversation, no matter the questions they have. Every mother I meet wants to be the one her son or daughter goes to with the difficult questions in life.

By the age of ten, children have learned how well their mothers can handle their questions. They've already observed their mothers' responses to less threatening issues and decided that the "big" questions will put Mom over the edge. So they keep quiet instead.

What message are you sending? If your child can't ask you the tough questions, perhaps you need to review whether you're maintaining the issue of respect in your relationship with him or her.

I heard of a fourteen-year-old boy who was in the car with his mother, headed home from school. As they drove, the boy asked, "Mom, how does a woman have an orgasm?" Fortunately for this boy, this mom was rarely surprised by his difficult questions because he'd been asking them all of his life. However, she'd just been handed her most difficult question to date.

The mother proceeded to answer his question as honestly as she could in a manner she thought he could grasp. She then asked if he understood what she'd explained, and he told her he thought so. When she asked him if he had any further questions, he said he didn't at this time.

As the mother continued driving, she became lost in her thoughts until her son said, "Thanks, Mom!" Not thinking about the previous conversation (she'd forgotten it rather quickly), the mother responded, "For what?" The boy replied immediately, "You didn't blink when I asked you the question."

Clearly this mother had established a relationship of respect with her son—one in which he knew he could ask her anything. She didn't go down interrogation lane with judgment and questioning, wondering why he wanted to know the answer.

She knew her son and respected their relationship.

He knew his mom and trusted she would take him seriously.

Years later, when this son was in college, he and his mother were still able to talk openly about sexual issues. The two of them established honesty and openness throughout his life because his mother gave him acceptance and respect.

Isn't that every mother's heart?

Remember, it is never too late to begin demonstrating respect toward your children. Even if you got off to a rocky start in their childhood and adolescent years, the reality of a mother respecting her adult child is a powerful, healing experience. Respect to an adult child says, "I revere you, regardless of where you are in your life."

Some of the greatest moments in my life have come when my own mother has shown me respect as an adult.

The decision to homeschool my son was difficult. I was in the midst of my career as a therapist—not at all prepared for God to direct me in this manner. Yet as you may know, God isn't concerned about our convenience. His concern was Taylor's best interest at the moment.

My anxiety about homeschooling encompassed several issues.

First, anyone who knew me would never have pegged me as a homeschool mother. I wasn't the type. The great homeschool mothers I knew were a cross between Mr. Rogers and Martha Stewart. They were accomplished at everything that made learning fun, with a heap of patience on top.

Second, I worried about being responsible for Taylor's academic achievements. The idea that his learning rested on my shoulders was overwhelming. If he didn't learn all he was supposed to learn, it would come back on me. I simply did not want to mess him up for life.

Third, and probably the greatest challenge for me on a personal level, was my anxiety about informing my mother of the decision. My mother was a public schoolteacher in her early years and went on to be a principal to physically disabled children. She was working on her doctorate in education at the time I was making this decision about homeschooling. Though we'd never spent a lot of time on the topic, I was unsure how she would respond. She was a big believer in education, and as a mother and grandmother, she exposed her children and grandchildren to many educational opportunities.

When I called my mom, I was a little nervous. While I was a confident person in my own right, I was wading into her territory, and I greatly trusted her opinion. I picked up the phone and proceeded to convey the recent series of events that brought me to my homeschooling decision. I then quietly waited for her response:

> *"Cathy, you're an excellent mother. If this is what you think is best for Taylor, then I think it is a great decision. Just let me know how I can help you!"*

That moment was one of the highlights of my life.

Her comment affirmed both my motherhood and my heart for my son. Her words told me she believed in me completely. My mother believed in me. That moment truly is one of the greatest gifts I ever received.

While it was within her character and our relationship for her to have confidence in me, it meant so much for her to affirm me as a mother in such a significant life decision. She did not let her own experience or background interfere with Taylor's best interest or my decision making. Her respect gave a young mother (me) confidence to proceed into an unknown world.

Most of all, children long to respect their moms. They want to be proud of her and feel as if she is comfortable in her role as their mother. They want to talk to her and to know that she recognizes that being a mother means being a mother, not their friend.

They long for Mom to
    draw the line,
        enforce the rules, and
            make the tough calls.

Here's a great example.

I was a part-time guidance counselor at a private Christian school for several years. During my last year, I taught a religion class once a week for the eighth-grade students. Because my daughter was in the class, I had an opportunity to become quite familiar with the girls in the class and their families. I had a front-row seat to understand some of the kids, their behavior and attitudes—and their hearts.

One day, in preparation for a teaching on unconditional love, I asked the kids to write down all the things they liked about their parents on one side of the chalkboard, and all the things they didn't like on the other. I was especially curious to see the responses of the two most popular girls.

Early in the year I had discovered these two who were the leaders of the class, outgoing and influential. Both of them were popular, smart, and athletic. Though they'd each struggled with rules ear-lier in the school year, both seemed to be finishing eighth grade on solid footing. I was curious to see what they would write.

As the exercise unfolded, I noticed the two girls were at differ-ent ends of the boards writing down their dislikes. With so many kids in between them, it was impossible for them to see what each other wrote down. In fact, their lists had few similarities. But there was one glaring common denominator.

Both fourteen-year-old girls wrote, "I wish my mom would be my mother instead of my friend."

Fast-forward about two months to the athletic banquet at the end of the school year.

This was one of the few events where the girls could wear clothes other than their uniforms. It was also a time when some of us teachers and counselors held our breath, because many of the dresses and skirts seemed a little on the short side. In spite of the admonishment to dress appropriately, some girls just had to test the limits.

While I was sitting at one of the tables waiting for the evening to get started, one of these two girls came over to me. "Mrs. Hickem, is my dress too short?" I asked her to turn around for me so I could see her. "No, Beth, it's absolutely lovely. You look wonder-ful. The length is perfect!" A smile came over her face, and she was relieved. Beth thanked me and went back over to her table and sat down next to her mother.

So the question surfaces, "Why didn't she ask her mother that question if her mom was with her at the banquet?"

The answer was on the chalkboard in the classroom two months prior. Her mother had been her friend instead of her mom, and she'd learned that her mother could not be counted on to do motherly things or give her needed boundaries and guidance. Her mother had ingrained herself as an equal, not a respected authority for her. Thus, she turned to a person she didn't know well but respected to get the blessing she really wanted from her own mother. It isn't that I was all that special. It was simply that I was comfortable in my proper role.

Teenagers long for someone in their life to respect and trust, someone who knows her role in that child's life. They need us to take our rightful place so they can turn to us at any time. They don't need another girlfriend.

They want us to be mothers.

It's called respect.

It's our job.

Our children and teens want us to display confidence. They will internalize our steadfastness when they see we really believe in our role as their mother. While they may not agree, comprehend, or understand, they will truly respect the position you take because you're standing for something and for *someone* you believe in.

When you are intentional about being your children's mother, they won't always like you. But they certainly won't respect you if you're their friend. They can get over not liking you. Just give them a few minutes or hours. But respect is a lifelong issue. It takes a lifetime to build but only minutes to destroy.

It's All in the Delivery

The most common denominator in learning to impart respect is how we go about delivering our message. This part gets a little embarrassing.

Let's be honest with each other.

Haven't you found yourself talking to your kids in a way you would *never* speak to an adult? If they're under two years of age, then it doesn't count. Come back to me in ten years and let me know if you have made it through motherhood without increasing your voice decibels!

One of the biggest ways we fail to communicate respect to our kids is how we speak with them, especially our teenagers. Our voice is powerful and it says more than words.

It communicates attitude.

It reveals our heart.

It creates walls or bridges.

All by how we say what needs to be said.

Even if we're right, we need to recognize that how we deliver our message is key to our kids' receptivity to the message we seek to deliver.

Have you ever listened to yourself?

Would you dare let yourself be recorded in the midst of talking with your kids about something when you're in conflict? If not, then you know the truth about yourself.

I openly admit that I've had decibel ranges to my voice.

I've swung from the fan blades like Tarzan.

I am guilty of reacting instead of acting.

At times my then-adolescent son said to me, "Mom, when you calm down, we can finish our conversation." That made me so mad because (1) I knew he was right, and (2) my son was acting more mature than I was.

My exasperation with his logic (or the lack thereof) often sent me over the edge. But the minute that happened, my effectiveness as a mother flew out the window. I always made a bigger impression when I handled myself as an adult.

I also discovered that my voice *intonation* was revealing. If I was sarcastic, curt, or impatient, that raised the level of the conversation to another stage of intensity and usually made things worse. Instead of calming things down, I could inflame the issues. Regardless of whether I was right to set my boundaries, enforce my rules, or define my expectations, I could negate everything by how I said it.

My body language, my voice intonation, and the look in my eyes all communicate either my respect or lack of respect for my children. If I want to be an intentional mother and I want my message—whatever it is at the time—to be effective, I must realize that I will have greater impact when I deliver my message as a whole package.

1. My heart needs to reveal itself in my voice.

2. My respect needs to come through in how I use my body to communicate.

3. My eyes need to say, "I don't like having to do this, but I will because I love you so much!"

Beneath it all, intentional mothers are called to create a safe atmosphere where opinions can be expressed and heard, feelings shared, and conflict resolved. Those processes will never be exemplified in a home where respect isn't a lifestyle.

Our children may or may not be happy. But our children will be healthy if we maintain our position in the way we respect them and live respectfully before them.

When we keep our eye on the big picture of what is right for our kids, and have less concern about receiving their approval, we become the kind of mothers that have no regrets when we look back on our children's lives.

Intentional mothers know that by keeping their focus on the appropriate priority, their children receive the best and biggest of God's blessings.

⚜

FAITH POINTS

"But if anyone causes one of these little ones who believe in me to sin, it would be better for him to have a large millstone hung around his neck and to be drowned in the depths of the sea."

~ Matthew 18:6 ~

I know what it is to be in need, and I know what it is to have plenty. I have learned the secret of being content in any and every situation, whether well fed or hungry, whether living in plenty or in want.

~ Philippians 4:12 ~

God has given us a tremendous responsibility in raising children. Part of that responsibility is to guide them in learning how to live a contented and upright life. As we mother them, our children not only listen to what we say but *how* we say it. Even more than that, they watch how we respond to people and circumstances. Our example will either teach them how to live well—be content, and love and respect God and others—or it won't.

1. What is the difference between contentment and happiness?

2. How do you show respect to your children? How do your children show you respect?

3. When is the last time you really listened to your child? What happened?

RAISING YOUR CHILDREN WITH *No Regrets*

4. Listen to yourself the next time you speak to your children. What tone of voice did you use? Did the way you spoke seem respectful or not?

5. What was the greatest insight you gained from this chapter, and how can you put it to use today?

6

The Difference between Control and Intention

Principle 6: Be Intentional about Being Intentional

In fall of 2006, news hit the airwaves and the Internet around the world—a mother and father lied to their adult daughter and took her away under false pretense the day before her wedding. They told her they wanted to spend the day with her, pick up her bridal gown, and take her to lunch.

Instead, they drove her five hours away from the town where she was to marry, crossed state lines into another state, and caused her to miss her own wedding—on purpose.

All because they didn't want her to marry her fiancé.

All because they didn't trust her.

All because of a word we spell C-O-N-T-R-O-L!

Control is a huge issue in our culture, in our churches, in our work, in our families. Our human nature drives us to seek to control as much of our lives and relationships as possible. With so much out of control in our world, no wonder parents try to protect their children by controlling as much as they can around them.

The problem is, control usually becomes less about protection and more about power. Then life can begin to spin out of control.

Have you ever been to a Little League game where parents are out of control? They yell at the umpires, coach the coaches, and push their kids to do better. Their conduct is obnoxious and provides a frustrating and bad example of adulthood. Clearly, many of these moms and dads have unresolved issues about their own athletic history and thus project their unfinished business onto their kids. It is a sad and pathetic sight.

But before we become overly critical of out-of-control parents, we need to turn our attention to controlling parents.

Unlike moms who lose it on the ball field, some mothers seek to control by reeling in whatever gets in the way of their child having, being, getting, or achieving the mother's definition of her child's success.

"Control queen" moms can completely undermine their well-meaning hearts' desire for their children.

The concept of control is typically associated with codependency, which develops in a person as a child if his or her environment feels emotionally unsafe. A child can feel vulnerable in many different ways, and even in families where you'd least expect it.

Control is no respecter of persons. It runs throughout all socio-economic, religious, racial, and educational backgrounds.

Being raised in a home where the adults are unpredictable, needy, addictive, and/or unstable sends a message to the child that no one is in charge. The result of such an environment is a child who feels inadequate and anxious. To compensate, the child seeks any means possible to calm the inner turmoil, to control the situation:

act out,
     withdraw,
          regress,
               or overcompensate.

Children raised by a controlling parent quickly learn the triggers that stimulate a reaction from the mother or father, so they expend tremendous energy trying to avoid these triggers. Instead of simply being children, such kids spend so much time developing avoidance behaviors for their mind and life that they grow up too quickly.

This disconnected growth pattern creates a child who, somewhere along the way, experiences consequences in his or her emotional development. Trust, self-confidence, trusting one's judgment or instincts, and one's view of life can all be impacted when a child comes from a controlling home life.

Control is also manifested in families where approval is paramount and insecurity is normal. It becomes a driving force when a mother reacts to others' opinions of her children rather than trusting her own. Such moms are guided by an approval addiction, leaving their children's welfare to strangers instead of in the care of one who knows them best.

I recently met with a mother who struggles deeply with control issues. The greatest manifestation of this problem is that she will do whatever it takes to please her friends or her children's teachers. She has really good instincts, but she grew up in a controlling home herself. As a result, she learned two defensive behaviors:

perfectionism and the need for approval.

When she and her husband arrived in my office, the entire family was in turmoil. The marriage was bad, the children were completely out of control, and chaos reigned everywhere. I thought it important to have their oldest child tested because he demonstrated some severe behaviors. I wanted to rule out any biological disorder or learning problems before we proceeded.

His tests results clearly indicated several factors we needed to consider.

First, the child had an IQ of almost 140—near genius.

Second, while the tests revealed a few areas of concern, nothing indicated that he should be acting out with such extreme, out-of-control behavior. My conclusion was that he'd learned to respond to the controlling environment in which he was being reared.

As I delved into the family history of the two parents, it quickly became obvious that the greatest obstacle to peace and harmony in this family was the issue of control.

Mom and Dad both came from families where expectations were impossible to meet but approval was the highest priority. Rigid ideation about children further impacted their ability to get their hands around their own children's needs, thus the out-of-control behavior from their son.

People will turn anxiety into control because it is an external way to calm internal chaos.

Control provides a false sense of safety, because people believe that if they control the variables in a given situation, the world will be a safe and wonderful place. This is an illusion, of course, but it is one that most of the world has bought.

This is especially true for mothers.

Most mothers struggle with control, yet they're often oblivious to it. They see themselves as simply being vigorous about impacting the outcome of their children's lives.

They want to see their kids' needs met.

They want to see their kids happy and successful.

The problem is the mothers' methodology, not their heart.

A controlling mother typically loves and adores her child. Her motives are pure and her desire is to bless. The downside is, she seeks to control the outcomes of situations for her children rather than modeling and teaching them what they need to learn.

There's a better, healthier way to mother children without all of the negative side effects of control. It starts by learning the difference between a controlling mother and an intentional mother.

FEAR OR FAITH?

Controlling mothers are fear-based mothers. They make decisions out of fear and live with the eternal "what if" questions. Parenting this way creates a constant environment of anxiety and stress for children. Living fearfully undermines confidence, reduces energy, and leaves mothers with an emptiness that cannot be filled.

Fear is a terrible characteristic to pass on to your children.

Because children are so sensory, especially when they are little, they read their mothers well. Thus, a child can sense fear in his mother's face, in her voice, and by her behavior.

He knows when a mother is hesitant to leave him with a new babysitter.

She senses when Mom is anxious about her behavior in school.

Kids recognize the signs of fear, even before they're able to communicate it.

When my daughter was a baby, she quickly connected to me emotionally. My husband, Neil, was senior pastor of a church when Tiffany was born. The church members loved her, and because her daddy was the pastor, they felt as if our kids were theirs.

I was uncomfortable with my child being passed around to everyone in the church, because I didn't believe it was in her best interest. Unlike my son, who never met a stranger, Tiffany was quite selective in whose arms she comfortably went.

As I observed my daughter, I noticed that she did not go to people with whom I was uncomfortable. She was only several months old, so it was impossible that she comprehended anything I said to her.

She simply sensed my discomfort and reacted accordingly.

A mom will battle fear in her heart throughout her motherhood journey if she remains in a control-dominant pattern of life. She will be quick to imagine the worst and go out of her way to have back-up plans for every possible outcome.

Fear can damage any type of child, but certain personality types are deeply scarred by a fear-based mom.

When fear dominates,
    hope is dampened,
        and that is sad for any child.

Intentional mothers break free from a fear-based lifestyle because they choose to live in faith. They embrace a sense of purpose and anticipation of God's blessings in their children's lives. While they recognize the challenges that lie ahead, they see them not as obstacles to be controlled but as opportunities to see God work.

Mothers who embrace their faith truly sense that God is bigger than anything their children will encounter.

When a mother lives intentionally, she makes choices instead of being a victim. She refuses to give people too much power for she knows that fear leads down a path marked by angst and frustration. She believes that "in all things God works for the good of those who love him";[1] she knows that her greatest obstacle to victory is probably herself, not her children.

A mother who wants to live a faith-based life instead of a controlling one will need to take a moment to examine her journey through childhood. Remember, there are only two reasons to ever look back: (1) to recall the faithfulness of God and (2) to learn from the past.

When a mother looks back to see how God worked in her life, she may not always be aware of the many times God stepped into her life and changed it in some way.

If her path was filled with love, opportunities, friends, and meaningful memories, she is blessed and can be thankful.

If her life has been full of difficulty, then she will need to take some time to reflect on the lessons she gained from those experiences.

How did these experiences impact her?

What does she do differently as a result of those painful life lessons?

Asking these questions often provides insights into how those challenges and hurts of her life weren't wasted.

Intentional mothers who are free from fear are great role models for their children.

They exude confidence and aren't afraid to fail.

> They know their value isn't in what they do but who they are.

> > They embrace their children in spite of themselves and recognize their value is based solely on God's view of them.

This fearless approach to motherhood allows moms to meet their children's needs without their own insecurities getting in the way.

DEVELOPING TRUST

Another key difference between a controlling mother and an intentional mother is the issue of trust. Trust is second only to love in the "need categories" for our children, and it begins immediately after birth.

The minute a baby is born, the formation of trust begins.

Attentiveness to the baby's needs,
> emotional presence with the baby,
>> affirming communication with the infant . . .

. . . all lay a foundation of trust for a newborn. As the child's life unfolds, parents will have many opportunities to strengthen the bond between them.

Trust involves respect and is necessary for a healthy relationship to exist during the coming adolescent years. Trust is developed over the course of the relationship and comes in handy when life doesn't make sense. In such times, trust may be all we have to hold on to. However, parents can't make the mistake of thinking they deserve trust simply because they're the parents.

Trust, like respect, must be earned.

I once met with a father who planned to separate from his wife. They had two children, ages five and seven. Although I did not support his decision, I felt it necessary to minimize any damage to his children as much as possible. So I explained to this dad the process he needed to follow that would demonstrate honor and respect to his children.

He was a little surprised at my recommendations.

"Why do I need to talk to my five-year-old about my decision?" he questioned me.

"Because your child needs to hear from you that your decision has nothing to do with him," I explained. "It proves you respect him enough to look him in the eye and tell him that his life will be different. If you want him to trust you in the future, you can't run out on him now without talking to him first."

This father took my counsel and did as I suggested. Then his five-year-old boy asked him, "Why are you making a bad decision, Daddy?"

If a child can understand that his dad's decision is a bad one, he can somehow comprehend that he is being taken seriously.

When a mother has control issues, she has trust issues. She struggles to trust herself, her children, her family, professionals in her children's lives, and most of all, God. Because of her own background, she sits on a fence of doubt, not wanting to commit herself. She struggles to trust anyone for any reason, believing that she or her children will be wounded or scarred.

This attitude has a high price and interferes in the relationships she values most.

Probably the most damaging consequence of a mother who doesn't trust is how it affects her. She doesn't trust her own judgment about her children, so she may take advice from strangers before she follows her own instincts.

Through the years I've observed that most mothers are pretty intuitive to their children's needs when they listen. I believe God created woman with a discerning heart, but mothers who struggle with control and trust are less likely to trust that intuitive sense.

When a mother doesn't trust herself, she struggles to trust her kids. She often projects onto her children—especially daughters—her own history of poor decision making, impulsivity, or deception. This damaging behavior sets the child up for a self-fulfilling prophecy.

When I was a guidance counselor at a middle school, I knew a precious young woman who was incredibly special. Jessica was every mother's delight, diligent to be her best at everything she did. She even possessed a maturity of faith marked by reflective and prayerful daily study, because spending time with God was so important to her. She was kind, tender, talented, bright, and conscientious.

One day Jessica entered my office, and the minute I shut the door, she began to sob.

"Mrs. Hickem, why does my mother not like me?" she cried.

I knew her mother to be strict, but I did not know there was such tension between them. I asked her why she thought her mom felt that way.

"No matter what I do, what I say, and or what I accomplish, my mother always assumes the worst about me," Jessica sobbed. "I've never done anything to cause her to not trust me, but she doesn't. I just want her to like me."

I attempted to talk to Jessica's mother, but her walls were rather high. I began by commending her good job in raising such a fine daughter, and commented that she must be proud of Jessica.

The mother said, "Thank you," then added, "You just never know when things will change." When I asked her if Jessica had ever given her any reason not to trust her, she replied, "No, not yet!"

I wanted to shake this mother and tell her that if she continued believing this about her daughter, Jessica would "live down" to her mother's low expectations. But at that point, I knew the only thing I could do while Jessica was in school was to be a refuge for her and continue to pray for both the daughter and the mother.

Fast-forward two years. I received a phone call from Jessica's father. The daughter was now in tenth grade and things were worse at home between her and the mother. I was no longer at the school, so the father had to hunt me down to seek my counsel. He was in tears.

"I don't know what to do. I am losing my daughter because my wife is suspicious of everything she does. The tension is so bad, and I am afraid if something doesn't change, I am going to lose my daughter," said this distraught dad.

I shared with him my observations from two years back and asked if he thought his wife would be open to addressing the issues.

"If I bring this up, it will be all over because she will think I've sided with Jessica," he replied. "As it is, when I point things out that I believe are unfair, it creates tremendous tension between me and my wife."

I told him that if he didn't do something, he would lose his daughter. I prayed with him, and he hung up, crying with a heavy heart.

Fast-forward three more years. My son saw Jessica when he came home from college.

"Mom, I saw Jessica tonight and you would not recognize her," he told me. "She is obviously not the same person we knew years ago. She is living a rough lifestyle now. She dresses loose, lives loose, and decided against college. She has a hard edge."

I was so sad for that young girl I had held in my arms so many years earlier, wanting her mom to simply trust her, and more importantly, like her. All of this was the result of a mother who could not trust her daughter because of the issues she failed to work through in her own life.

Controlling mothers will pass down the curse of mistrust unless they heal from their own emotional wounds. Regardless of what created trust issues for a mother, it is her responsibility not to let them get in the way of her children's lives.

The first step is awareness of where she wants to be.

Intentional mothers handle their trust issues by trusting Christ first. They recognize their own struggles and choose to go to the One who is trustworthy. This is a challenge for many mothers, but intentional moms know that if they let go of their own control and risk trusting God, they will be rewarded for it.

RELYING ON GOD

When a mom trusts God, she finds peace in the midst of the storms of motherhood. She believes nothing she and her family will face is bigger than God. She is willing to go on a wild ride and know that she won't fall off, no matter how fast the turns come at her.

Intentional mothers have a safe and loving view of God. They believe He has their best interest at heart and wants to meet their needs. They see that behind the "rules" some people call Scripture is God's heart of protection.

Most of all, an intentional mother trusts that God knows her children better than she, and that He will be with them all the times when she cannot.

A year ago, my son prepared to go overseas to study abroad. Although he was twenty years old at the time, it was still difficult for me to think about him going away to a foreign country for more than four months, knowing absolutely no one.

Taylor had to take everything he needed in one suitcase, which was a challenge. I asked him if he wanted some assistance with preparations for this trip, and he said it would be great if I came. So I traveled to Houston, where he was living, to help him prepare for his trip.

Our time together flew by fast. Knowing he was going to a part of the world that had just experienced the tsunami, I bought him dog tags to wear for identification. We took care of some legal matters and enjoyed being together while we worked.

On my trip home, I realized I was being asked to trust God again. I thought back on all the other times God had taken care of Taylor when I wasn't around, and I could sense God reminding me that He had not changed in His ability to do it again.

Although I was in Houston only forty-eight hours, God put me in touch with some friends I had not seen in several years. During my brief visit, they reminded me they had lived in Hong Kong and promised to e-mail their friends and let them know of Taylor's impending arrival. On top of that, one friend would be going to where Taylor was studying—not once, but twice during the time Taylor would be there—so he could check on my son for me.

In these practical ways, God showed me how He would watch over Taylor for me.

There's no greater way for women to bless God than to trust Him with the treasures they value most: their family.

When mothers choose to trust, they experience peace.

When they choose to release their kids into God's hands, the responsibility for how their children develop doesn't feel so heavy and burdensome.

Imagine if you had the lead engineer of the world's largest computer company at your beck and call, 24/7, including holidays. If you're like me, a computer novice, you'd soon be on a first-name basis with this genius. (I have just enough experience to be dangerous.)

You'd be awed to think that there'd be no problem this genius couldn't help you solve. The fact that this computer guru would drop everything to help you with your little computer issue when he or she had an entire corporation to run would be humbling. It would also be a great relief!

That is how it is when a mother actively trusts Christ. She sees that the One who created her children is on call 24/7 to help her with them. She knows that because God engineered them, there will be no surprises to Him.

She can count on God to give her the hints, signs, and cues she needs to meet her children at their deepest places of need. She will rest easier knowing that if she stays connected to God, He will help her be the mother her children need whenever they need it.

AVOIDING PRIDE

Control has another dirty side: pride. It is a characteristic we all struggle with now and again. However, pride is one of the most common arenas where control surfaces in our motherhood journey. If you don't believe me, listen in on a group of new mothers talking about their babies. You'll hear jealousy, competition, and rivalry between mothers who also happen to be best friends.

So what could mothers compete about when their children are this young?

How well the baby is sitting up by himself?

How soon the infant begins walking?

Heaven forbid one of them refuses to walk until he's fifteen months old!

Pride is our attempt to cover insecurity.

Nothing brings out a mother's insecurity more than her children, especially when they misbehave.

Think about the times you wanted to slide under a table or hide under a rock. These feelings likely were connected to a moment when your son picked his nose on stage or your daughter decided the checkout line at the grocery store was an ideal place for a temper tantrum.

Does any of this resonate with you? Don't feel alone, but don't get too comfortable either.

Controlling mothers mistakenly think that when their children act out, it reflects on their ability as a mother instead of understanding such moments as signs of where their kids are developmentally. When a child is disobedient, he is simply doing what children can and will do at that age. All children have days when they test the limits, don't feel well, or just act ornery. It is called *normal human behavior*.

If your child never demonstrated moments of this nature, you would have cause for concern.

These demonstrations are not, however, a reflection on you.

Children don't come prepackaged or programmed. We, the mothers and fathers of the world, are called on to teach them manners, values, faith, respect, and self-control. It is our responsibility to guide, educate, model, correct, and encourage our children in the lessons of life. These aren't one-time lessons but multiple opportunities to instruct our children on the ways we believe healthy people live.

Most mothers want their teaching moments to stay within the household where no one can see them correcting their children. But that isn't realistic.

Children don't consult a mother's social approval scale to schedule the best time to challenge Mom. Those moments simply happen when they happen.

So why do mothers become horrified when their children act like children?

Perhaps because they see it as a reflection on themselves. Controlling mothers fail to recognize the attention needs to be on the child and not the mother. When a mother makes such moments about herself, then pride takes over, and she's already lost the battle with the child.

When she seeks to control out of pride, she probably won't make the best choices for her child either. Adding herself to the equation weakens her child's potential for learning. Mom is "in the way." Her pride will dilute the situations designed for her child to deepen his trust in her. Pride also diminishes the opportunity for the mother to better understand her child.

Pride keeps the focus on us, which leads us to be selfish. Selfishness leads to idolatry because our focus isn't on God.

When we get to that place in our lives, everyone is in trouble.

Intentional mothers focus on their child. When they can do so in the midst of difficult moments, their kids will walk away the better for it. Whatever the disciplinary action might be, learning occurs, and the bond between mother and child is strengthened.

Parenting is about our kids, not us. When we let that truth sink in, we become more effective in our discipline and our communication. By being intentional, we're keeping the child a priority, which allows us to experience a deeper awareness of God and His desire for us to teach our children about Him.

Intentional motherhood frees mothers from getting sucked into a battle they cannot win. It helps keep their focus on the emotional and spiritual health of their children. It also gives mothers the desire to be teachable. The wall of pride is no longer around their heart, and the stubbornness that accompanies pride dissipates.

Intentional mothers know they need help and aren't afraid to ask for it. They realize the best position they can be in is when they throw up a prayer that says, "I can't mother this kid, Lord!"

That is not a prayer of despair but of wisdom.

It is an acknowledgement that we're in over our heads and in desperate need of help. We are telling God we trust Him. It is the best move we can make, because He has all the answers we will ever need.

Resentment vs. Confidence

Finally, intentional mothers recognize that the greatest danger associated with being a controlling mother is the potential for control to plant rebellion and resentment in the heart of a child or teen.

When mothers dominate their children and fail to slowly loosen the reins in their children's lives, trust is destroyed, self-confidence is weakened, and bitterness surfaces.

While that outcome isn't the desire of the mother's heart, the end result is the same. To an adolescent, control says that Mom does not believe in the core of who that teenager is.

Let's get something straight. I am not saying that teens should be in charge and make all the decisions.

I am saying that parents must understand their job is to teach their children and adolescents how to make decisions. This process takes place over time, with practice. The only way for that to happen is for parents to provide the opportunity for their teen to learn, practice, and even have the chance to fail—not try to control every situation so the child doesn't have the chance to decide anything.

Children and teens need to know their family is a safe environment in which to make mistakes. There's an old saying: "If you can't do something right, then don't do it all."

I think that adage is wrong.

It reinforces the message that one must be perfect or else not bother.

The saying we adopted around our house was, "Anything worth doing well is worth doing poorly until you get good at it!"

Our goal at the Hickem home was for Taylor and Tiffany to enjoy exploring different experiences and opportunities, not to be fearful of trying.

Many adolescents from religious homes rebel because they've been overly restricted and dominated by well-meaning but controlling parents. The parents thought if they kept a tight harness on their kids during the high-school years, their teens would conform to the parents' standards and expectations.

Unfortunately, this isn't true. Especially when control takes the place of explaining the reasoning behind a parent's standard or value. Controlling only creates clever kids who outsmart, lie, and deceive their parents.

Control is an insult to another person because it says, "You don't have the ability to make good decisions without my help." That underlying message erodes the hope, confidence, and joy of growing up.

I once had the privilege of working with a brilliant young woman. In addition to her intelligence, this high-school student was an outstanding athlete in several sports and had a heart of gold.

One day during a session, she said something I thought was very insightful: "I am so tired of my parents trying to control my every move. I need to make some decisions for myself, because it is going to be really scary when I get to college if I haven't had any practice."

She hit the nail on the head.

She recognized the issues for what they were. Fortunately, her mother heard her, and they made important progress.

Intentional mothers keep a broad perspective of their role as mother and understand that releasing their children is part of the job. They know mistakes will be made along the way, but because their pride isn't involved, they have an easier time addressing issues appropriately.

Intentional moms increase their likelihood of reaping honesty, depth of character, and confidence in their teens because they understand their goal isn't to raise perfect, overprotected kids but to develop their children from the inside out, with all the confidence God placed within them.

Faith Points

"No one will be able to stand up against you all the days of your life. As I was with Moses, so I will be with you; I will never leave you nor forsake you."

~ Joshua 1:5 ~

Control is another word for mistrust. It is saying that we're certain we have *the* answer and that other people will hurt us. Most of all, it denies the role Christ desires to play in our daily experiences with our children. Christ never controlled His followers. He led them and was laser-focused on loving them well.

1. Do you ever struggle with the issue of control? If so, how does this affect your children?

2. How does fear impact the way you mother your children?

3. Can you think of a time God showed His faithfulness to you? How can you teach that same faithfulness to your children?

4. How has your pride gotten in the way of acting in the best interest of your child? If faced with a similar situation, how could you handle it in a healthier way?

5. What was the greatest insight you gained from this chapter, and how can you put it to use today?

7

GOD'S SENSE OF HUMOR BEGINS
WITH CONTRACTIONS
Principle 7: Be Intentional about Being God-Dependent

Carrie entered my life as a young Christian psychotherapist looking for a mentor. She had been married to David for three years. She was quick to tell me she had no interest in being a mother but that she would love to volunteer for our motherhood organization.

For the next nine years, Carrie spent a lot of time with me, my daughter Tiffany, and our ministry volunteers. All this time she kept her resolve to remain childless, yet she often spoke with me about it because she worried that her lack of desire to be a mother was a reflection of selfishness. I advised her to stay focused on what God was presently doing in her life and trust that if He wanted her to be a mother, He would change her heart.

One day, Carrie called me to say that God had indeed changed her heart. Soon she was pregnant.

Carrie and Tiffany had developed a special bond over the years of our ministry travels. As a result, she asked my daughter to come to her home three hours away and stay with her before the birth and a couple weeks after the baby arrived.

Carrie is a bubbly, outgoing young woman who loves life and knows God. I find her precious, with amazing spiritual maturity. Carrie is also fun, insightful, and admittedly a little spoiled. Like a lot of women, she prefers getting her way, even in childbirth.

As Carrie's pregnancy proceeded, she arranged her birth plan—determined to have an epidural. Every time she attended birthing class or spoke to her doctor, she reiterated her desire for a pain-free delivery. She fully expected things to go as planned.

Because this was Carrie's first child, she anticipated a minimum of ten to twelve hours of labor. She also thought the baby would come after her due date; she'd been told first babies were usually late. Her fantasy was that she would begin labor, David would calmly drive her to the hospital, she would get her epidural, and the baby would arrive pain-free.

Remember the word *fantasy*.

Here's the reality. A couple days before her due date, David left for work and Carrie began having mild cramps. She called her physician's office, and the nurse told her to come in, but told Carrie she was probably in false labor. Tiffany was already at Carrie's house, so she and Carrie headed to the doctor's office, convinced they would soon return home.

After being examined, Carrie learned that her baby was indeed on its way. She called David to tell him the news, and Tiffany quickly drove her to the hospital.

Tiffany is usually calm under pressure; however, in this situation, my then-nineteen-year-old immediately began to respond like a typical nervous father. Had the ride to the hospital been any farther, the trauma of the car trip may have caused Carrie to deliver the baby in the car!

So much for the calm ride to the hospital.

The minute she arrived, Carrie began asking for the "drug doctor" (the anesthesiologist). She told everybody she saw that she was to get an epidural, but apparently no one was listening. Things were definitely not going as she'd planned.

David finally made it to the hospital (after a frantic trip home to get Carrie's bag and pillows) and reassured her that everything would be okay. Carrie told him nothing would be fine until she received her epidural. By this time, she was no longer her sweet self. She'd become a wild woman.

Carrie continued pleading for an epidural, but the nurses kept telling her, "We have to get your IV in first and draw blood before we can administer the epidural."

After two hours of their trying to draw her blood, Carrie looked like a pincushion.

With each passing minute, Carrie's pain became more unbearable. She was literally begging for the epidural—*screaming* is a more accurate description.

Suddenly her nurse responded, "Honey, we don't have time for an epidural now because we've got ourselves a baby coming, and she is in a hurry." The doctor confirmed the nurse's observation, and Carrie and David's daughter, Elleri, arrived twenty minutes later.

Carrie's' labor lasted only two and a half hours instead of twelve. There'd been no calm car ride with her husband to the hospital. Elleri entered the world early instead of late. Worst of all, Carrie got no epidural.

Carrie's introduction to motherhood was totally opposite from her "plan." Though she'd tried to control the circumstances surrounding her daughter's birth, Carrie soon saw her perfect plan disintegrate. She could not control how her daughter entered the world. Yet this unexpected delivery was only preparation for the rest of the journey she will share with Elleri, David, and God. Her predictable life became a faint memory. Carrie had just entered the "no-control zone" of motherhood.

My friend Carrie's journey into motherhood is a typical scenario for many women who experience childbirth. They start the process calm and in control. By the time the baby has arrived, they've learned one of their first lessons of motherhood: *control is an illusion.*

Adoption is a similar experience. The only difference is how the lesson is taught. In birthing children, there is physical pain. In adopting children, there is emotional pain—and the absolute awareness that you have no control whatsoever.

Having experienced both roads to motherhood, adoption was definitely more frightening and vulnerable. The birth parents determined how high or low our experience would be. My husband and I could do nothing to impact whether or not we would be parents. We had absolutely no control. Fortunately, we still had our faith in God and a strong support system as we walked through this helpless process.

But isn't helplessness the point?

Once Eve blew it, God created the birth process with the intention of teaching us that we needed help.

The challenge of a child's entry into the world is God's first lesson for mothers. There's no such thing as control, and birth gives mothers a front-row seat to that truth, whatever form it takes. Unfortunately, most moms do not see beneath the moment to the deeper life lesson.

Here's the real lesson in the birth process: The reason the lifelong journey of motherhood starts off on such a rocky, unpredictable road is to teach you to be God-dependent early in your journey as a mom. The earlier you learn to depend on God, the more you like your children, the more you enjoy being a mom, and the less you care about other's opinions on how you perform as a mother. Doesn't that sound wonderful?

God knew that the way to a woman's heart was through her children. From the beginning of time, women have been the caretakers and primary nurturers of children. The child's dependency creates a deep sense of protection and responsibility within us. It is a power that seems to arrive at the same time the baby does.

In my work as a therapist, I've sat on a task force for women's prison ministry. What I've learned about women in prison is that you never turn your back on them. By the time these women enter prison they're hardened and bitter. Most of them have been sexually, physically, or emotionally abused, and have lost hope in anything and anybody. The walls around their hearts are ten stories high.

However, if you find *any* crack in their protective wall, it appears when you ask them about their children. A tear may trickle down their cheek, or a tiny smile may start to surface when this part of their heart is stirred. Mothers, free or imprisoned, are vulnerable to their children in a way that nothing or no one else compares.

God created us this way because He knew He could teach us the greatest lessons of life, faith, and unconditional love through our children. He knew nothing else could get our attention quicker.

Throughout this book, you have heard the theme that raising children is the single most difficult job in the world. Nothing compares to the intricate challenges that come with each child's special and unique creation.

Motherhood is a challenging journey; God made it such so that it could be much easier if we recognized the part He wanted to play in it. Partnering with God to raise children into wonderful young adults is even more His desire than ours.

Can you imagine He could love them more?

GOD-DEPENDENT MOMS

Being God-dependent means trusting God with your children. It means listening to the thoughts that pop into your head that allow you to know that no matter what you see or feel, He loves them more and will be with them when you can't. When these thoughts come to your mind, and they're accompanied by peace or comfort, recognize them as God's spirit speaking to your heart, giving you guidance and counsel on how to proceed. It means learning to hear God's voice speak to your heart and head so you can find peace when you have no answers.

When Taylor was sixteen and Tiffany fifteen, I signed them up for a weekend course on etiquette—two half days of learning all the intricate details of formality. While I didn't expect them to be in tux and formal gown frequently, I thought the class provided a good refresher as they approached young adulthood. I've always believed that manners communicate powerfully to prospective employers and in-laws. Most important, I believe good manners make a statement to the world about what a young person thinks of him or herself, as well as others.

The day before the class was to begin, I woke up on a Friday morning from a dream in which Taylor was killed in a car accident. Upon awakening, I reflected on the dream and realized that Tiffany would be affected by the accident as well, because she is almost always in the car with Taylor.

Over the years, I've learned that when such dreams come, I have two choices: fear or faith. I can either live in dreaded anticipation of something awful happening to my children, or I can seize the opportunity to pray and trust God.

That Friday morning, I decided on the latter.

The organization I worked with was having a charity golf tournament that day. On my way to the golf course, I called two of my prayer partners and asked them to begin to pray for my children until I felt the threat was over. They both agreed and began to pray for protection for my Taylor and Tiffany.

As the day went on, I went about my business of networking, relationship building, and having fun. As I rode from hole to hole on the golf course in my cart, I prayed, thanked God for all my blessings, and enjoyed the beautiful south Florida day.

Night came and I still felt compelled to pray fervently for my kids. Taylor had a football game that night, so I knew they would not be home until late. While it would have been nice to have them home, to be assured of their welfare, I could not cave into fear. It was important that I give them room to live their lives. I will tell you, though, I was relieved when they walked in the door.

The next morning I continued to pray. About 11:30 I finally felt a release. I sensed that I had completed what God wanted me to do for my children in the wake of my dream.

I was peaceful.

An hour later I answered my phone and heard Tiffany crying hysterically. It took me several minutes to calm her down, only to discover that she and Taylor had been in a car accident on the major interstate in our area. I immediately headed for my children.

Upon my arrival, I saw cars strewn everywhere across the highway (thirteen cars, to be exact). But I also saw both of my kids, standing outside a totaled car with both of their friends—unharmed.

As I assessed the situation, I clearly recognized that God's hand was on my children, especially Taylor. While Taylor was giving the police his version of the accident, another car began sliding out of control across the highway and headed right toward them. Had they not jumped out of the way, both would have taken a direct hit.

The policeman also told me that the occupants in our car should have been injured, given the type of damage the car sustained.

I've no doubt that the accident would have had completely different results had God not led me to a place of faith through prayer.
Had I simply responded in fear, I believe my early morning dream
would've turned into every mother's nightmare. Regardless of the
outcome, I knew I had done my part by fervently praying for my
children. I could look back on that circumstance with no regret.

When mothers are intentional, they learn to lean on God for parenting wisdom, hope, insight, and strength. They also find themselves more confident in the daily challenges of being a mom. The
weight of the motherhood responsibility isn't as heavy because
they know God carries the load for them. They recognize that the
more they depend on Him, the more they trust Him with their
life, and their children's.

RELEASING OUR KIDS TO GOD

Another benefit of being God-dependent is that we reach the point
of expecting God to take care of our children. This becomes in-
stinctual—a way of thinking and believing about our kids where
we automatically turn to God first in all issues involving them.
Trusting God this deeply with our kids is liberating for mothers.
They truly feel as if they are in partnership with Him in the process of raising their children.

As we experience this close, dependent relationship with God, it
becomes easier for us to release our children to Him.

God knew what He was doing when He started us off with infants
instead of teenagers. When children are tiny, we recognize clearly
their total dependency on us. We're protective, careful, sensitive,
and attentive. We know they can do absolutely nothing for themselves, and we don't expect anything from them. We completely
accept them, colic and all.

That dependency captures a mother's heart and causes her to invest everything she is into this tiny new life. From the moment a
baby is placed in her arms, a mother makes a choice about whom

she will trust for answers, truth, and direction in raising her new child. Aware of her own limitations, and knowing that no one will ever love her child in the same manner, she is faced with what should be an obvious choice. Still, every new mother's choice is impacted by her own journey with the family that raised her.

It would be so nice if trusting God were a simple decision. On the surface it appears to be a no-brainer. But several key variables affect how and if a mother can trust God with her children.

When a woman grows up with a critical mother or father, she perceives God in that same light. If her parents ignored her when she was growing up or constantly communicated their disappointment in her, she will see God in that same light.

On the other hand, if her mom and dad demonstrated unconditional love, believed in her in spite of her mistakes, and spent time with her, she will trust God more readily. In her heart she already will have learned the blessings of a tender parent-child relationship. It is easier for that mom to transfer her trust onto her God—her heavenly Father.

Stop and think about it.

What are your trust issues with God?

Do you see any similarities between the way you perceive God versus how you perceive your mother or father?

In my counseling through the years, I've had the privilege of hearing a lot of pain, thoughts, struggles, fears, and needs. One consistent observation I can make is that people transfer their early parental relationships onto their heavenly one. I've also found this to be true for people who weren't particularly religious or spiritual. Their earthly journey impacts whether they can even consider that someone bigger than them exists—someone who could possibly love them.

Whether we transfer a positive understanding of God from our parents' influence or have to overcome a negative perspective of God, once we learn to trust God with our lives, we recognize the relationship between love and trust. When we realize that God loves our children more than we ever can, we know we can trust them to His care. He loves them enough to place His new creations in our lives, and in so doing, He blesses us with the opportunity to experience the incredible gift of a parent-child love relationship. When we depend on God to be our parenting partner, we can more easily let them go, knowing their Creator holds their lives in capable, comforting, loving arms.

Over the years I've had the privilege of working with many birth mothers who've given up their children for adoption. I always have the most profound respect for them because I know their sacrifice is out of love for that child and concern for his or her future. One of the truths I share with these moms in the wake of their difficult, heart-wrenching decision is very comforting to them:

While a child may not always be in the birth mother's arms, he or she will always be in her heart.

As a result, one of the gifts a birth mother can give her child is to pray for that child through the years. It is the ultimate display of dependency, because she cannot actively touch her child, make decisions for him, or nurture him in a motherly sort of way. But she can trust God with him and bring him up often in her thought life and conversations with God. She can change the outcome of her child's life by releasing him completely to the God who created him.

For moms who have the privilege of raising their children, letting go and trusting is at least a daily experience, if not a moment-by-moment one. It would be nice if we could do it once and it lasted forever. But the truth is, we must make the choice daily. By consciously choosing to release our children to God day after day, we're reminded how much we need Him to help us parent our children.

My daughter had some health problems during her senior year of high-school that threatened to deter her from attending the college of her choice. She didn't get a release from doctors until May, which, as many of you know, is too late for most college-bound kids to change their mind.

Tiffany had been accepted into the school of her choice, but because of her health issues, she'd turned down the acceptance. Now, at the last minute, she was free to start her freshman year there, but fall classes were full. So the university offered her the option of starting classes that summer semester. This meant we had only three weeks for all the arrangements to fall into place.

When God is involved and in control, the details fall into place.

In three short weeks, Tiff went from being a high-school student to living alone in a condo, hundreds of miles away from home. She'd never stayed by herself before, much less live alone, but this was the path to fulfilling her dream.

When I walked out of the condo leaving my youngest behind, I was strong and courageous. I knew this moment would be one of the hardest in our relationship because we both knew life would never be the same again. I also felt vulnerable because Tiff was truly going to be alone.

Alone.

Just saying that word makes me shudder when I think of my kids.

But leaving her in the condo that day was just another opportunity for both of us to practice what we'd been preparing for all her life: to trust God.

I knew that from that day forward, Tiffany was totally in God's hands.

Whether you're cradling an infant in your arms or saying good-bye as your child leaves for college, God wants you to know He is worthy of the honor that comes with trusting Him with your children. When you share your heart with God and say, "I can't do this thing called motherhood anymore!" you will probably hear His sigh of relief. He won't fight you or play tug-of-war for your child because He is a gentleman God. When you finally let go, He will step into your life and the life of your child.

WATCHING GOD WORK

Have you ever felt sorry for your children because they had to undergo experiences that were a direct result of choices you made or were made for you? Have you ever tried to overcompensate for things that seemed unfair? Have you had moments where you thought your children might feel deprived because times were challenging or difficult?

If so, God just handed you an enormous opportunity to let your kids participate in an adventure where they get to see . . .

> the impossible become possible,
> the amazing become real, and
> their faith take root.

When mothers choose to live a life of faith, trusting their children to God, they'll find the path rich with experiences that will better prepare them and their kids for life. Learning to wait graciously, asking for what you want or need, and expanding the way answers are delivered can be huge moments for increasing a child's faith and hope. We don't want to hinder God's mysterious unlimited ways.

Have you ever watched a small child's eyes when they see someone blow bubbles?

They're fascinated, curious, and excited. While they don't understand the chemistry behind the bubbles, they don't care. They simply relish the experience.

When children and teens run into life experiences they don't understand, we're not to feel sorry for them. What might look like disappointment or disadvantage may actually be God's way of protecting our children or teaching them a valuable lesson they will need later in life. Too often moms and dads get in the way of opportune moments for children to see God work in the daily experience of their lives.

Once there was a family who was going through a difficult time financially. They didn't have money to buy groceries on a weekly basis, so the mother had to buy them every one or two days as a little money came in.

One day she returned from buying $25 worth of groceries, and her husband asked her if she had bought soap. "I ran out of money because I needed all of it to buy food. We were out of the basics, and I just couldn't buy anything else," said the mom.

The husband began to complain and wondered what he would do about not having soap.

"If you need soap, I suggest you take it up with God," she replied. Their two children heard this exchange and laughed.

The next morning the mother went outside to retrieve the Sunday paper. Wrapped with the paper was the largest bar of soap she'd ever seen. In addition, there was a coupon for another bar.

When she went in the house, the kids saw the soap. "Hey, Mom, God sent Dad some soap!"

The kids were so excited they immediately took the bar of soap to their dad. They thought it very cool that God heard their dad's prayer for soap.

This is one of hundreds of stories that can surface in a family when they remain focused on faith instead of circumstances. Crises are great opportunities to demonstrate . . .

> steadfast faith,
>> gentle patience,
>>> and incredible peace.

All because you allowed a difficult moment to become a platform for children to see God show up in the life of your family.

Intentional mothers know and trust that if God allows a difficulty to enter your children's lives—or even affect the entire family—He plans to use this experience as preparation for their future. He may use challenging circumstances to develop their character, patience, perseverance, or faith, but God always has purpose and a plan.

Nothing is wasted in the divine economy of life.

Circumstances do not define us. What we do with them does.

Every trial or challenge is an opportunity to return to the basic question of our faith: What do I believe about the nature and character of Jesus Christ? About God?

Recently a young woman was talking to her mother, telling her that someone had asked her if she was anything like her mom. She'd answered her friend:

"As often as I can be."

Then the daughter told her mother that she was amazed at the depth of her mother's faith and tenderness when she knew how hard life had been and how many losses her mom had experienced in life. This young woman said she didn't believe she would ever possess her mother's greatness.

This mother knew that her daughter's journey was an incubator in which God would prepare her for what lay ahead in life. There was no way this mother could know the exact plans God had for her child. But she did know God had allowed this young woman to observe faith in action through a mom who was truly committed to knowing God at every level.

All the challenges and sacrifices won't be wasted.

Not for your kids or mine.

When our children and teens watch us become God-dependent, we teach them it is okay to be vulnerable, to ask for help, and to allow ourselves to have needs. They realize that we don't have all the answers, which makes it easier for them not to have all the answers either. Simply put, our God-dependence demonstrates to our kids that when we are weak, He is strong.[1]

Children who haven't been protected from life will be far more equipped and prepared for whatever life throws at them. They will have the knowledge that God is big, faithful, and incredibly powerful when they feel little, overwhelmed, and scared. They will know so because they watched their mother—who was intentional in trusting God instead of herself—live out her faith and not simply talk about it.

Does it get any better than that?

"I have no greater joy than to hear that my children are walking in the truth."[2]

FAITH POINTS

But this happened that we might not rely on ourselves but on God, who raises the dead. He has delivered us from such a deadly peril, and he will deliver us. On him we have set our hope that he will continue to deliver us.

~ 2 Corinthians 1:9–10 ~

The most amazing relief we can get is to let go of the burden we sometimes feel as mothers. God never intended us to carry the weight of this incredible responsibility on our shoulders. His desire was to carry it for us, live through us, minister to us, and love us. When we release our load and rely on God, He helps us lead our children to rely on Him and discover His purpose for their lives.

1. In what areas of your children's lives do you have the most difficulty trusting God?

2. How can learning to trust God more in your life help you trust Him more with your children?

3. Why is it so difficult for so many mothers to release their children? How can you overcome the resistance to let them go?

4. What are your children learning about God from watching you? When and how have you recently seen God at work in your children?

5. What was the greatest insight you gained from this chapter, and how can you put it to use today?

THE BEGINNING AND
THE END OF THE STORY

A few days before Thanksgiving one year, I was returning from a weekly radio program I hosted. The station was about forty minutes from my home, and I still had a lot to do to prepare for the holiday.

I was traveling on one of our main highways when a car suddenly pulled out in front of me and I T-boned it. My air bags went off, smoke poured out of the car, and I was stunned. I felt stinging pain through my entire body.

Within a few minutes, police arrived on the scene and an ambulance followed shortly. I was placed in the ambulance and taken to the hospital, leaving my totaled car behind. At the hospital, emergency personnel quickly examined me. Fortunately, I had not sustained serious injury. But it didn't feel that way to me, based on the pain I was in.

I was lying in an ER bed, in agony, when my mother appeared from behind the curtain. Hers was the sweetest face I could have seen at that moment. Here I was, forty-three years of age, and I could finally let go and cry because my mother was with me. I didn't have to be strong anymore.

No matter how old I get, I will always long for my mom's

comforting touch,

gentle way, and
total acceptance.

You may or may not have that type of mother—comforting, gentle, and accepting—but you can *be* that type of mother . . .

. . . if you are willing to see what God sees when
He views your children.

THE NEVER-ENDING STORY

Every mother I meet eventually brings up a universal topic of conversation—the time when her children will leave home. Some moms dread the day. Others look forward to it with anticipation and joy. All somehow think they will breathe easier and life will be less hectic with no kids around the house.

But the truth is, when your children finally leave the nest, it's not the end of your job. Your mothering days are just getting started . . .

. . . in a new and different way.

Last summer, my college-age daughter returned home for the summer, and I observed some of her money management techniques I thought she should evaluate. I didn't want to control her but to encourage her to discover some lessons on her own.

As her mother, I wanted to be respectful of her stage of growth as a young woman and not meddle. However, I felt the responsibility of helping her grow in this area. So I left her a note one morning with some questions to explore regarding her finances.

When I returned home later that day, she walked into my bedroom and handed me a folder, saying, "Mom, I got your note and I spent several hours reviewing my finances and reflecting on what I learned. After you read this, I'd like to talk with you about it."

In her letter, after she summarized what she'd discovered, she ended with this:

> *I'm sorry for not being diligent or determined where my finances are concerned. I will not sit idly by anymore.*
>
> *I hope you will take the time to look at this and then talk with me about it. I sincerely want to discuss this with you and get your input on what can change and how I can improve.*
>
> *I love you and appreciate your generosity with my lifestyle but mostly with your wisdom. I know few mothers who would have the time and patience to help get to the core of my habits and lifestyle and not see this just as a problem for now but also as a learning tool to help me for the rest of my life.*
>
> *I love you mostly and most,*
>
> *Tiffany*

As you can imagine, I was touched and grateful by the heart of her letter. It confirmed once again that two decades of investing in my daughter and of seeing her life from a broader perspective had created a trust between us that allowed me to continue to speak into her life. She saw that I was not merely interested in solving an immediate problem; I truly wanted to prepare her for the future. The essence is, she trusted my heart for her. The process of our life journey together kept her heart teachable in moments like these.

For a mom, the story is never over. You will be a mother the rest of your life.

Before you get exhausted just thinking about that, take comfort in knowing that while motherhood does not stop, your role changes and so does your responsibility.

Rather than relying on you for instruction, for daily direction and basic life requirements, your kids will need you for different things once they leave home. Regardless of their age, your adult children will always need you—to believe in them, study them, and give them room to grow.

They will need you to . . .

> love the people they love.

> recognize their right to make mistakes without giving your opinion.

> intentionally trust that God is bigger than any choices they make.

Sometimes it may not seem as if your children need you, and you'll have to make adjustments in how you mother them after they grow into adulthood. Some mothers find this to be a trying time because they don't understand why how they parented their teenaged kids no longer works.

Your relationship with your kids is changing now, and that means your mothering must change. But it doesn't mean mothering becomes less intentional.

By now you've learned why being intentional is critical to healthy parent-child relationships. The same truth is valid as your kids move toward adulthood. When you remain intentional when your children become adults, you . . .

> optimize the blessings they receive—from both you and God,
> offer them a source of wisdom and hope,
> and leave a legacy of love and acceptance.

But your legacy is the end of the story. Let's go back to . . .

The Beginning . . .

If you have made it to the conclusion of this book, hopefully you have also embraced the idea that we mothers must be intentional with our children. Some of what you've read in these pages rang true for you, so you're probably experiencing a shift in your thinking about the most important relationships in your life.

So let me ask the obvious question.

Do you know the number one reason we should be intentional?

It's because God set the example. He's intentionally parented His children since the beginning of time.

That's right. It's that simple. We need to be intentional because God is intentional, and has been since He created life.

At the beginning of this book I defined intentional as "sharply focused or fixed on something." When we realize that God was "sharply focused" when He created us and had a purpose in mind for each person, with an outcome to match, we can begin to appreciate the example He set before us.

God created mankind with one purpose:

To be in relationship with Him.

God wanted us to know Him and trust Him. He loved us from the beginning, and He demonstrated this by creating us in His image. God loved all His creations, but when He created humanity, we were different.

We were like Him.

As a result, He created a perfect place to birth His first two children—Adam and Eve. He gave them everything they needed or could possibly want. He provided for them, set boundaries with them, communicated clearly to them, and began a loving relationship with them. He was intentional in being the parent they needed.

Yet we all know their story. Things changed. God's children took matters into their own hands and blew it, so much so that the rest of us are paying for it to this day. It just goes to show that no matter how "perfect" a parent is, children always make their own choices and decisions.

God loved them enough to give them freedom to choose—even to make the wrong decision—even though they chose to disobey.

Here is the point: God had a plan to give His children the world, but they didn't receive it. Still, that never deterred Him from continuing a relationship with them and meeting them where they *were*, not waiting for them to get to where His heart longed for them to be.

From Adam and Eve, move forward in time to Noah and see how God was intentional in leading him and his family. Noah was already five hundred years old when God told him to build a boat in a town that had no water in front of a people who'd never seen rain. For the next hundred years Noah and his three sons worked on this boat.

God was intentional with Noah because He used him to save the world from the flood. God had a plan, and Noah carried it out as he was told.

After Noah the stories keep going about people God intentionally loved. And in each case, He parented them in ways that reflected their particular God-created personalities. Abraham, Moses, Isaac, Joseph—God lasered His love and purpose toward each one. And that's just the book of Genesis! There are sixty-five more books illustrating how God outlined His intentional purpose for people.

Moving beyond the Bible, we can identify people throughout history whose lives—both the challenges and the successes—impacted the world, changed the course of the past, or caused humankind to search for something more. We see the purpose in their existence. They were created for that moment.

God created every person on earth—from Adam and Eve to you and me—with a godly purpose, and for his or her particular moment in life.

If you are a mother, you were created for this moment.

God intentionally allowed you to be right where you are, with the children you have been given, so you could become more and more like Him.

After all, God's heart for all of us is that we be a reflection of Him.

It is God's heart for your presence in your kids' lives to be a blessing, a source of wisdom and hope, and a keeper of the vision He holds for each of them.

And when you are an intentional mother, your children reap the benefit of a mom who's maintained a Kingdom vision, believed in God, and believed in her children. Your children's faith can then be a blessing to generations to come.

Think about it. If you want to leave a legacy with the greatest value, shouldn't you choose to be "sharply focused" on those relationships where you can make the greatest heart investment? Doesn't it make sense that if you keep your eye on the goal, you will arrive at your destination with no regrets?

By the time we reach the end of the story, we see God had no regrets about creating you and me. If God did so for Himself, it is His desire that we live—and mother our children—the same way.

We will make our mistakes. We will be imperfect mothers and have imperfect children. But if we are intentional . . .

. . . we can raise our children with no regrets!

FAITH POINTS

For he chose us in him before the creation of the world to be holy and blameless in his sight. In love he predestined us to be adopted as his sons through Jesus Christ, in accordance with his pleasure and will—to the praise of his glorious grace, which he has freely given us in the One he loves.

~ Ephesians 1:4–6 ~

We are God's children. Our gift from Him is that He has modeled for us a great example of an intentional parent. He has a plan, and He has been working it since the beginning of time. Sometimes His kids don't cooperate with Him, but that doesn't change the course He has set to be the perfect example He is. What example will you leave for your children?

COACHING PLAN

"Coaching" is a plan and process that allows parents to set goals in a realistic fashion and then outline the steps to accomplish those goals. The coaching plan is a way of being accountable to learn from what you read while not being overwhelmed. It helps mothers break issues down into manageable pieces so they can make progress and create change in their lives and families.

Coaching will ask you to look *forward* toward the behavioral and attitude adjustments or daily life changes you want to make. Don't look *back* at your failures. Think forward with a new sense of faith and hope and remember that change takes time. Be patient with yourself and with your children. You will be amazed at what you learn about yourself, your children, and God.

The following coaching plan will help you put the principles of *Raising Your Children with No Regrets* into practice. Feel free to copy these pages and create a new coaching plan for each principle. Don't try to tackle everything all at once. Try making a plan for one principle a month. Take the time to set your own goals and steps. Then celebrate each accomplishment!

COACHING PLAN

Start Date: _____

1. Set Your Goal

Identify an issue in your parenting that you would like to change.

_____

_____

_____

_____

a. Toward whom is this change geared? A particular child . . . or all of your kids? Explain.

_____

_____

_____

_____

b. Does the change involve your child changing . . . or will your child change when you change? Explain.

_____

_____

_____

_____

2. Plan for Your Goal

How will you know when you have accomplished your goal? This answer will help you define your goal.

_____

_____

_____

3. Write Your Goal

Write out your goal. Be specific.
Example: I want to be more encouraging for my kids.

_____

_____

_____

4. Action Steps

Identify what steps you need to implement in order to reach your goal. Remember to make small, realistic steps for each of the next four weeks. Don't set yourself up for failure. Spaces for several steps are provided for you, if needed. Use spaces only for steps that are directed toward your goal.

Week 1

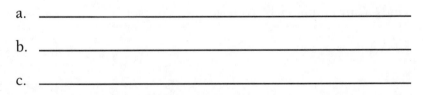

a. _____

b. _____

c. _____

Review at the end of the week and check off those steps you accomplished. You may carry a step or two over to the next week.

Week 2

    a. _____

    b. _____

    c. _____

    Carryover step _____

Week 3

    a. _____

    b. _____

    c. _____

    Carryover step _____

Week 4

    a. _____

    b. _____

    c. _____

    Carryover step _____

5. Evaluate Your Goal's Purpose

How will achieving your goal enhance your relationship with God? Your child(ren)? Your view of yourself?

God _____

_____

_____

COACHING PLAN

Child(ren) _____

_____

_____

_____

Self _____

_____

_____

6. Write Your Prayer

Write out a prayer that shows God your dependency on Him to achieve your heart's desire. Be sure to thank Him in advance for His faithfulness to change you.

_____

_____

_____

_____

7. Goal Accomplished: Celebration!

How did this change impact your child(ren)? _____

_____

_____

_____

_____

How did this change impact you? _____

_____

_____

_____

How did God reveal Himself to you? _____

_____

_____

_____

What is the most important insight you received from this experience?

_____

_____

_____

Additional Resources

Web Sites

www.intentionalmotherhood.com is the official site for Intentional Motherhood, an organization founded by Catherine Hickem. At this site you can sign up for Catherine's monthly newsletter, which is inspiring and insightful; check for Intentional Motherhood events coming to your area; order additional resources, including *The Heart of the Matter Is the Heart of the Mother*, a mother's enrichment Bible study written by Catherine Hickem; learn more about Catherine and her organization; and contact Catherine or the organization with questions or comments.

www.noregretsmom.com is the official site for this book. Here you can tell us your personal story of how the *principles of intentional motherhood* have impacted you and your parenting. We welcome and encourage you to participate. You can also sign up for the monthly newsletter; check for Intentional Motherhood events coming to your area; order additional resources, including *The Heart of the Matter Is the Heart of the Mother*, a mother's enrichment Bible study written by Catherine Hickem; learn more about Catherine and her organization; and contact Catherine or the organization with questions or comments.

COMMUNICATION TOOLS AVAILABLE ON OUR SITES

DISC Personality Profiles: Allow parents to identify the way God wired their children so they can more effectively relate, discipline, teach, and love their kids. (See Intentional Motherhood Web site—www.intentionalmotherhood.com—for information on obtaining the following DISC profiles for your use.)

- *All about BOTS, All about You!*
  Designed for use with children from kindergarten through elementary school. As you work through this book with your child, you will learn how God has wired his or her personality. This deeper understanding can help you to more effectively relate, discipline, teach, and love your child. You will need one book for each child.

- *Get REAL! . . . Who You Are and Why You Do Those Things*
  This personality development handbook for teens includes a self-scoring profile assessment. Teens can identify their own, unique personality style. They can discover for themselves their strong points and identify the areas in which they need to improve. It's not so hard for them to improve relationships at home and with friends when they better understand themselves and others.

COMMUNICATION TOOLS AVAILABLE THROUGH YOUTH & FAMILY INSTITUTE

The following communication resources are available from Youth & Family Institute, Augsburg College, 1-877-239-2492.

Faith Talk
Designed to provide meaningful sharing of memories, activities, specific events, and value-forming experiences of faith for small groups of people. Includes forty-eight discussion cards in each of four categories. Ages ten and up.

Faith Talk for Children
Not a game but a tool to assist children and parents or other adults to have meaningful conversations as they share stories. Includes twenty-four cards in each of four categories: Memories, Growing Together, Actions and Feelings, and Wondering. For all ages.

BOOKS

I've found these books to be particularly helpful at different stages of my motherhood journey.

Boundaries: When to Say YES, When to Say NO to Take Control of Your Life, rev. ed. Henry Cloud and John Townsend. Grand Rapids: Zondervan Publishing House, 1992.

Bringing Up Kids without Tearing Them Down: How to Raise Confident, Successful Children. Kevin Leman. Nashville: Thomas Nelson Publishers, 1995.

Confident Kids. Robert G. Barnes Jr. Wheaton, Ill.: Tyndale House Publishers, 1987.

Dare to Discipline. James C. Dobson, PhD. Wheaton, Ill.: Tyndale House Publishers, 1970.

Emotional Intelligence: Why It Can Matter More Than IQ, 10th anniversary ed. Daniel Goleman. New York: Bantam Books, 2005.

Grace Walk. Steve McVey. Eugene, Oreg.: Harvest House Publishers, 1995.

Holding Time: How to Eliminate Conflict, Temper Tantrums, and Sibling Rivalry and Raise Happy, Loving, Successful Children. Martha G. Welch, MD. New York: Fireside Books, Simon & Schuster, 1988.

The Hurried Child: Growing Up Too Fast Too Soon. David Elkind. Reading, Mass.: Addison-Wesley Publishing Co., 1981.

Is This Your Child? Discovering and Treating Unrecognized Allergies. Doris Rapp, MD. New York: William Morrow and Co., Inc., 1991.

The Power of a Praying Parent, rev. ed. Stormie O'Martian. Eugene, Oreg.: Harvest House Publishers, 2005.

Sacred Parenting: How Raising Children Shapes Our Souls. Gary L. Thomas. Grand Rapids: Zondervan Publishing House, 2004.

The Way They Learn: How to Discover and Teach to Your Child's Strengths. Cynthia Ulrich Tobias. Colorado Springs, Colo.: Focus on the Family Publishing, 1994.

MOVIES

Sometimes movies are a great tool to capture a message because you can see the lesson lived out in life situations. The following movies will give you a clear perspective on how your family issues can interfere or bless your children. These movies are not to be viewed as a family but for you or you and your spouse to watch, as parents who enjoy learning through a visual means. Seek ways to apply the lesson to improve your mothering or benefit your family's relationships.

Dead Poets Society (1989): This film is a great example of a parent whose control issues permanently interfere with his child and how that affects his son's well-being.

Facing the Giants (2006): This movie gives a powerful portrayal of fathers who truly believe their kids when no one else might.

Ordinary People (1980): Pay attention to the pain of the mother's emotional wall and how it wounds and damages her son.

The Sound of Music (1965): Watch this classic from a parenting perspective. Notice how the children are fearful of their father and how he is fearful of feeling for them. The nanny allows the children to blossom by allowing them to become children once again.

What a Girl Wants (2003): View this movie from the perspective of how important a father's acceptance of a child is to the confidence of that child.

You undoubtedly will recall other movies or see new ones that contain a nugget of truth regarding how you can be a better intentional mother. Look at these films not only for their entertainment value but also for what truth might apply to your own motherhood situation.

ENDNOTES

Introduction: A Mother's Heart

1. Linda Ellis, "The Dash," 1996.

2. *American Heritage Dictionary Online*, s.v. "regret," http://www.bartleby.com/61/72/R0127200.html (accessed November 14, 2006).

Chapter 1: Why Well-Meaning Moms Raise Insecure Kids

1. *The Motherhood Survey: Fresh Insights on Mothers' Attitudes and Concerns* (New York: Institute for American Values, 2005), 20.

2. Ibid., 14.

3. Ibid., 28.

4. Ibid., 20.

5. In most cases throughout the book, pseudonyms are used in place of real names.

6. *Motherhood Survey*, 21.

Chapter 3: You Can Live Peacefully in the Teenage Years

1. Claudia Wallis and Kristina Dell, "What Makes Teens Tick," *Time*, May 10, 2004, http://www.time.com/time/

magazine/article0,9171,994126,00.html (accessed November 14, 2006).

Chapter 4: Become a Thinking Mom

1. Daniel Goleman, *Emotional Intelligence: Why It Can Matter More Than IQ,* 10th anniversary ed. (New York: Bantam Books, 2005), 35.

2. Ibid., 35–36.

3. Ibid., 43.

4. Ibid., 43–44.

5. Matthew 16:18.

Chapter 6: The Difference between Control and Intention

1. Romans 8:28.

Chapter 7: God's Sense of Humor Begins with Contractions

1. See 2 Corinthians 12:9..

2. 3 John 1:4.

ABOUT THE AUTHOR

Catherine Hickem is a mother of faith who has had a personal relationship with Jesus Christ for almost forty years. As a result, she is passionate about challenging women to become the godly mothers He calls them to be. She understands the heart of a mother and gives women strategies to inspire, educate, and equip them in every phase of motherhood.

The various roles of Catherine's life give her credibility to speak on many topics with authority. She is a pastor's wife, mother of two college students, psychotherapist, certified DISC trainer, and executive coach in the corporate world. In addition, she is on the women's ministry staff of one of the largest churches in America. Catherine speaks for conferences, retreats, and events across the country. At home in Delray Beach, Florida, she is featured on a weekly radio program as "Mom Coach."

Catherine is founder of Intentional Motherhood, a national ministry to women, and author of an accompanying Bible study, *The Heart of the Matter Is the Heart of the Mother.* Her passion for the life application of biblical truth creates a hunger in a mother's heart to know God on a deeper level.

Catherine's career as a Christian psychotherapist has given her a front-row seat to share the intimate journey of women's lives. God has used this perspective to impart wisdom, deepen her faith, and further her resolve to share the power of Christ's transforming love with women.

ABOUT INTENTIONAL MOTHERHOOD, THE ORGANIZATION

Founded by Catherine Hickem, Intentional Motherhood is a non-denominational Christian organization that ministers to the needs, challenges, and hopes of every mother. Intentional Motherhood strives to inspire, educate, and equip mothers in every phase of motherhood to be confident and intentional in their lifelong parenting role. Through a variety of seminars, resources, and coaching programs, Intentional Motherhood partners with churches and community organizations to effectively reach women who are on a spiritual journey to raise godly kids.

To book Catherine Hickem for a speaking engagement or an Intentional Motherhood seminar, please contact 1-800-844-0711 or www.intentionalmotherhood.com.

TELLING YOUR STORIES

I hope that through the pages of this book you have gained confidence in your ability to mother your children without regret. My heart's desire is that, as you seek to follow God's example in being *intentional* as a mom, your relationships with your children will deepen and you and your family will receive incredible blessings.

If embracing the truth behind one of the seven principles of an intentional mother has transformed your mothering, your life, and/or your children's lives, we want to hear from you. Please send us an e-mail regarding which principle God used to give you a fresh, hopeful lesson and blessing and the result it brought to you and your kids' life journey.

E-mail us by logging on to: www.noregretsmom.com.